18 **HVH** 91

HARBOR VIEW

THE HOTEL THAT SAVED A TOWN

Story by: NIS KILDEGAARD
Photography by: ALISON SHAW

VINEYARD STORIES
Edgartown, Massachusetts

Published By: Vineyard Stories
508.221.2338 | vineyardstories.com

Design By: Bluerock Design
617.807.0240 | bluerockdesignco.com

Printed in China
Library of Congress Number: 2014932078
ISBN 978-0-9915028-2-0

Page 2: In a picture taken on August 26, 1896, the Harbor View is the backdrop for beachgoers.

Some of the Island's greatest charm is in the things it does not have. There are no hot land breezes. The average temperature is several degrees below that of the mainland. There are no poisonous snakes. There is no under-tow on the beaches, and there are no mud flats along the shore as the balance of the Island tides holds the swing from high to low water at a minimum. There is no smoke from factories or railroads, no weekend traffic jams, stop lights or roadside billboards.

FROM A 1940s BROCHURE ADVERTISING THE HARBOR VIEW

Table of Contents

INTRODUCTION

CRIMSON HOLLYHOCKS SWAY IN THE COOL BREEZE BESIDE THE BROAD
PORCHES OF THE HARBOR VIEW, THE OLDEST HOTEL IN THE OLDEST
TOWN ON THE ISLAND OF MARTHA'S VINEYARD.

Lilies and hydrangeas, beach roses, bluebell flowers, and purple butterfly bushes line the lawns, white fences, and brick sidewalks.

The round table under the Victorian cupola has attracted a gathering of five—two men in business garb, a woman, and two happy children wearing flip-flops and baseball caps. Sandwiches have been carried out from Water Street Restaurant, glasses of iced tea are perspiring lightly, and it's impossible to say where this little meeting lies on the long continuum between work and leisure. First, the men are earnestly engaged while the little girl enjoys her lunch, but then she clambers onto a lap to be bounced and rocked by—perhaps her grandfather?

Across the front veranda, the rockers, painted a lovely shade called Majestic Blue, are full—some guests reading the morning paper, others their tablets, still others sitting with paperbacks folded on laps, taking in the harbor scene. The absence of cell phone chatter is remarkable, and welcome. Off to the east, classic Doughdish Herreshoff sailboats skitter around racing marks in the outer harbor. Ahead the lighthouse gleams in the sun, its beach dotted with umbrellas, towels, and families at play. Off to the right, twin ferries ply the 527 feet between their landings on Daggett Street and Chappaquiddick. Westward lies the bustle of Edgartown, the village center so besieged with visitors in summertime.

Looking out from the shady porch, Donnie Ethier, the Harbor View's engineering coordinator, sees the hotel as a place that's both inseparable from Edgartown and slightly set apart. "Downtown Edgartown—there's people everywhere, just standing in the middle of the road," he says. "Out here, you're secluded away a little bit."

Yet at one moment in the Vineyard's annual Independence Day celebration, the past and present at this elegant old hotel converge. At that time, the paraders who have snaked their way through the back streets of the old whaling village of Edgartown turn from Thayer Street to Starbuck Neck Road and onto North Water Street, and they suddenly see the view that opens up to reveal the Harbor View on its promontory overlooking the broad expanse of the blue harbor.

It's a quintessential Martha's Vineyard moment, and it's impossible for anyone who has marched in that parade—and everyone eventually does—to imagine it without that breathtaking turn at the hotel that has, in many ways, defined the town and the Island where it has ruled for almost 125 years.

At that moment this story begins to unfold, when a town in desperate need is rescued by the sea, some rocking chairs, and people who dreamed big.

MAP OF EDGARTOWN
Dated 1889

In 1602 Bartholomew Gosnold, of Falmouth, England, . . . was the first Englishman to sail directly to the American coast.

He landed on a small island he called Martha's Vineyard. . . . The next day he landed on the larger island. After exploring it and finding it so large, well wooded, and with such luxuriant grape vines, many beautiful lakes, and springs of the purest water, he transferred the name and called it Martha's Vineyard.

The History of Martha's Vineyard
by Henry Franklin Norton

"[This island had] an incredible store of Vines, as well in the woodie part of the Island, where they run upon every tree, as upon the outward parts, that we could not goe for treading upon them."

John Brereton
Chaplain aboard the ship *Concord* that first landed on Martha's Vineyard.

1891

"Harbor View Bluff", Edgartown, Mass.

The original hotel, built at the edge of the settled village, is pictured in a panoramic postcard sold at the pharmacy of its owner, Dr. Thomas J. Walker.

THE END
OF DECAY

1891

Edgartown, once the home to the wealthiest whaling captains on Martha's Vineyard, had struggled with desperate poverty for decades, since the mid-century collapse of the whaling industry.

On the morning of Wednesday, July 1, a large flag with a white background, blue border, and the words "Harbor View" in crimson letters is run up the flagpole of a new enterprise at the very edge of Edgartown. Inside, at a handsome wood counter, manager J. V. Drew welcomes the hotel's first guests, Mr. and Mrs. George B. Elliott of Boston. For $2.50 or $3.50 per day, the Elliots will get three meals a day and a room with the latest in comforts and conveniences, including gas lighting, mattresses of horsehair and woven wire springs, and baths and toilets on each of the three floors.

They will, in the days to come, be entertained daily with concerts, shows, and all the marvels Edgartown has to offer—all in a setting that has a breathtaking view from a sprawling veranda.

That quiet transaction in the summer of 1891, and the welcoming and housing of guests at a resort hotel, is a moment Edgartown had been awaiting for decades.

The town's population plummeted by nearly half in just four decades, to a low of 1,156 in the 1890 census. Meanwhile, Edgartown residents watched enviously as neighboring Cottage City—later renamed Oak Bluffs—prospered as a resort, drawing thousands of people every summer.

Edgartown wanted what Cottage City had, a thriving resort economy based on the emerging American fashion of summering by the sea. There, what had begun in 1835 as

From atop the Old Whaling Church, a view to Edgartown and the harbor beyond.

"IT IS A PLACE FAR ADVANCED IN DECAY: OF ALL ITS WHALE-SHIPS, WHICH GOT FROM THE SEA THE HARD-EARNED FORTUNES OF ITS PEOPLE, THERE IS BUT ONE LEFT. THIS LIES UPON THE WAYS, STRIPPED OF ITS RIGGING, A MERE EFFIGY OF A LIVING CRAFT. . . . LITTLE BY LITTLE THE POPULATION IS DRIFTING AWAY; SOME HOUSES STAND EMPTY, AND THE QUICK AGENTS OF DECAY WHICH MAKE HAVOC WITH OUR FRAIL NEW ENGLAND HOUSES WILL SOON BE AT WORK AT THEM, AND EVEN YANKEE THRIFT CANNOT KEEP IT AWAY."

Nathaniel S. Shaler, 1874

Reported the Vineyard Gazette *on the week of the Harbor View's opening in July 1891:*

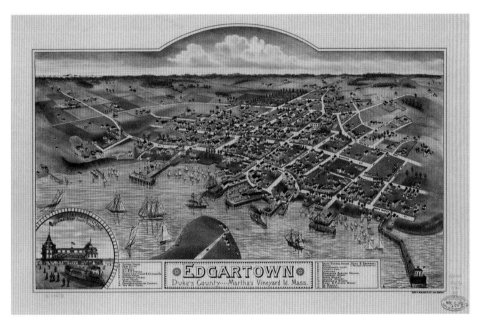

An artist's "birds-eye" sketch of Edgartown in 1886.

PHOTOGRAPHER R. G. SHUTE TOOK SOME FINE VIEWS OF THE HOTEL MONDAY AFTERNOON.

The finished pictures are now on sale at his store, samples to be seen in the window. Mr. Shute has been fortunate in securing extra fine results and has made a picture which every Edgartonian far and near will desire to be in possession of.

———— *Price* ————

50¢

EACH

a religious retreat under the oaks in a sheep field on land bordering Nantucket Sound had led to the development of a new resort that boasted small residential lots, curved avenues, and hotels for the visitors. A substantial new wharf made it ever easier to get to Cottage City. And by 1868, commercial areas were emerging that included a ladies' hair dressing parlor, bakeries, milliners, tailors, photographers' studios, and more. It was a developer's dream.

But the same was not true in Edgartown.

Harvard professor Nathaniel Southgate Shaler, writing an 1874 travel piece on Martha's Vineyard in the *Atlantic Monthly*, visited Edgartown and found signs of decline everywhere.

Charles Marchant (seated on left), editor of the Vineyard Gazette *at the time in their Edgartown offices.*

THE NEED DEFINED

"In conversation with a New York gentleman the other day, he casually informed us that he could no doubt direct fifty persons to Edgartown this summer, and would gladly do so, if the hotel accommodations were more ample; but that they were people, many of them, who wished to be together, would not object to paying a first-class price for first-class board and service, but would not submit to 'eating in one place, lodging in another, and doing all their smoking on the street.' We thought this was perhaps a trifle brusque, but, like every other fair-minded person in Edgartown, know that his statement contains a large amount of truth."

Vineyard Gazette, July 1890

The captain's houses along North Water Street in Edgartown, shown after the Civil War, when they had begun to fall into disrepair.

WILD WOMEN RUNNING THE STREETS AND AN EMPTY HARBOR SPURRED BUSINESS LEADERS TO PIN THEIR HOPES ON A NEW HOTEL.

An editorial in the *Vineyard Gazette* in 1864 described a shocking street scene outside its offices of "hideous yells" emanating from "a score or more men in pursuit of a half dozen filthy, dirty, ragged women who are a disgrace to their sex and to humanity."

Almost thirty years later, things were only getting worse.

Fear that their town—and, not incidentally, their livelihood—was collapsing drove town leaders to make a final stand. Sixteen local men, pooling their funds, decided to build a resort hotel of their own, one they hoped would steal the visitors from the hotels of Cottage City and deposit them in Edgartown, the first town settled on Martha's Vineyard.

And so, a few weeks after Mr. and Mrs. Elliott were greeted in 1891, the grand opening of the Harbor View drew hundreds of guests from across the Island and the mainland—an event heralded by the *Vineyard Gazette* as filled with "princely hospitality" and a moment that brought back the whiff of success to Edgartown.

A new era had begun.

Even with train service from the summer resort at Oak Bluffs, the Mattakeset lodge at Katama was a failure.

THEY HAD TRIED

Edgartown's leading businessmen were willing to invest in the push to reinvent their town as a summer resort, but their first efforts met with little success. Dr. Daniel Fisher, whose whaling fleet made him the wealthiest man in Edgartown (his 1840 mansion is a landmark on Main Street today), invested in 1872 more than $2,000 to help extend the Vineyard Sound Railway from Boston to Woods Hole. That year the citizens of Edgartown voted to lay a beach road from the bustling resort at Oak Bluffs. And in 1874 the taxpayers voted $15,000 to build a railroad from Oak Bluffs to Edgartown.

At the end of the new railway, on the Katama plains south of the village of Edgartown, another group of businessmen tried to duplicate the success of Oak Bluffs with a grand summer lodge, the Mattakeset, and a development of cottages around it. The transparency of that effort to copy another town's winning formula couldn't have been more obvious: E. P. Carpenter, director of the Oak Bluffs Company that had built the resort they so envied, was enlisted as chairman of the project, and the longed-for village of summer cottages was gridded out by Boston landscape artist Robert M. Copeland, the designer of Oak Bluffs.

It was clear almost from the beginning that the Mattakeset would not be Edgartown's tipping point as a summer resort. The lodge, with its seventy-five guest rooms and 125 feet of frontage on Katama Bay, opened in August 1873. Weeks later, the Panic of 1873, when banks collapsed all over the country, sent the nation plunging into recession. Only a few speculators bought lots around the Mattakeset, and no new city of cottages sprouted on the plain.

The Edgartown railway line, built on the sands along the new beach road and damaged each winter by northeast storms, ran its last train to Katama in 1896. The lodge hung on for a few years after that, closing for good in the fall of 1905. In 1910 the owners of the Harbor View Hotel purchased the derelict lodge for its lumber.

The Mattakeset had been an expensive lesson but an important one: Edgartown would not find its success as a resort by imitation, but only by recognizing and building on its own best assets.

The Mattakeset Hotel in its initial summer; it was a complete failure.

In his history, *Martha's Vineyard: Summer Resort,* Henry Beetle Hough, the longtime and famous editor of the *Vineyard Gazette,* summarized the town's predicament:

"WHEREVER EDGARTOWN MEN GATHERED TO TALK OF THE FUTURE, CONVERSATION CAME AROUND TO THE NEED OF A NEW SUMMER HOTEL, IN THE TOWN ITSELF. HOW ELSE COULD ANY GROUND BE GAINED OR HELD AS A WATERING PLACE?"

Right: A view to Starbuck Neck from Chappaquiddick, with the Harbor View at far right.

THE HARBOR VIEW WAS EQUIPPED WITH THE LATEST IN CONVENIENCES:

A telephone line to the nearby Holley's Livery Stable enabled guests to order teams without leaving the hotel.

DR. THOMAS WALKER
Town Doctor

REV. LUTHER T. TOWNSEND
Prominent Methodist Minister

JOHN L. MAYHEW
Leading Island Builder (No Photo Available)

A ROLL OF HONOR

Talk of a resort hotel in Edgartown turned to action when sixteen leading businessmen formed the Edgartown Hotel Company in August 1890. The enterprise was capitalized with $5,000—fifty shares of stock with a par value of $100 each.

Announcing this news, the *Vineyard Gazette* hailed the list of investors as "indeed a roll of honor," declaring, "The gentlemen who have displayed the public spirit and business sagacity, in at last taking hold of this hotel matter, are entitled to and will receive the approbation and good wishes of the entire community."

Three enterprising men—a cleric, a contractor, and a town physician—held half of the hotel company's initial stock and quickly emerged as principals in this new and exciting project.

Dr. Thomas J. Walker was both a town doctor and one of Edgartown's wealthiest men. As was common in the day, Dr. Walker also owned his own pharmacy, the Edgartown Drug Store, in the building on North Water Street that is now home to Murdick's Fudge. There he concocted, prescribed, and sold his own patent medicines, and his store sold postcard pictures of Edgartown taken by his wife, Myra, an avid photographer.

Reverend Luther T. Townsend was a prominent Methodist leader and one of Edgartown's first notable summer residents. He was on the faculty of Boston University, a lecturer at the Chatauqua School of Theology, and later president of Gammon Theological Seminary in Boston. A widely published essayist and speaker, he preached often from the pulpit of the Old Whaling Church. He was an investor in property both on Chappaquiddick and in Edgartown's village proper, including the land at Starbuck Neck where the hotel was built.

John L. Mayhew was one of the Island's leading contractors, with main offices next door to the Wesley House in Oak Bluffs. His investment in Edgartown's new hotel involved both labor and capital: he held stock in the company, and his men installed all the plumbing and gas lines in the project.

The location of the new hotel was appreciated as a primary asset from the start. The site lay on the outskirts of the settled town, in the pastures beyond North Water Street's grand row of sea captains' homes. Reported the *Vineyard Gazette*, "It is on the left of North Water st., the hotel grounds comprising about an acre of high land which the Hotel Co. recently purchased of the Starbuck's Bluffs Land Co. Set back from the street about 30 feet the hotel will face about southeast, with fine water and land views from every window."

THE HOTEL'S VERANDAS OVERLOOKING
EDGARTOWN HARBOR WERE PROMINENT
FEATURES. ITS DESIGN CALLED FOR
A 10-FOOT PIAZZA ACROSS THE ENTIRE
FRONT AND 45 FEET OF PIAZZA ON THE
SIDES, MAKING A CONTINUOUS PROMENADE
OF ABOUT 105 FEET. ROCKING CHAIRS
WOULD BE PLACED ON THE PORCHES TO
TAKE ADVANTAGE OF THE SEA BREEZES
AND THE VIEW.

A CIVIC ENTERPRISE

Through the winter of 1890 and into 1891 the people of Edgartown eagerly followed construction of the hotel. From the beginning, this project had the quality not of a speculative venture but of a civic enterprise supported by the community at large.

"The framing of one story is up, and the boarding of that will probably be completed by tonight," reported the *Vineyard Gazette* in December. "Masons are busy on the chimneys, and the work of digging the cellar under the rear extension has begun. With weather like that of the past three days the building will 'grow' very perceptibly during the coming week."

The new hotel's shingles occasioned excitement in January's news columns: "The shingles which are to be used on the new hotel are as handsome a lot as have been seen in town for a long time. They are originally from St. John, N.B. It is calculated that 100,000 will be used on the hotel building."

In April the plastering was finished, and a crew from the firm of Hobart & Butler set to finishing the carpentry work. Local workmen followed the carpenters with their brushes and buckets of paint.

J. V. Drew of Boston was announced in May as the Harbor View's first manager; he had managed the Hotel Naumkeag at Cottage City the season before, and through the winter he had been running a hotel in Crescent City, Florida.

The new hotel was furnished in June and readied for its inaugural 1891 season.

"We hear complimentary remarks on every hand for Manager Drew," reported the *Vineyard Gazette* that July. "The hotel, naturally, in the last two weeks has been visited by hundreds of our townspeople who are interested and curious as to all the details of furnishings, etc., and in every instance these visitors have been met with that quiet cordiality and courtesy which are characteristics of the model landlord and which will be appreciated the coming summer by the hundreds of guests who will find a home at the Harbor View."

As the new hotel was opening, Walker, Townsend, and Mayhew bought out their thirteen fellow stockholders for $8,000 and became the Harbor View's sole owners. They would hang on through the hotel's early financial difficulties, with ownership dwindling over the next two decades to two owners, then to one.

DINNER STARTED AT 9:45 P.M. IN THE DINING ROOM, WHERE, THE *VINEYARD GAZETTE* FAIRLY GUSHED, "PROBABLY ONE OF THE MOST RECHERCHÉ SUPPERS EVER SPREAD IN EDGARTOWN WAS SERVED." THE MENU FEATURED FILET OF BASS, LOBSTER SALAD, SALMON SALAD, POTATO PUREE, FILET OF BEEF NEAPOLITAN, PICKLED TONGUE, QUEEN OLIVES, BRAISED HAM, TURKEY, CHICKEN CROQUETTES, MASHED POTATOES BROWNED, SEVEN VARIETIES OF CAKE, TWO FLAVORS OF ICE CREAM, COFFEE, AND TEA.

A COMMUNITY GATHERING

The first party ever held at the Harbor View, a week before the grand opening, reflected the special place of this new business in the civic life of its community. The first reception and supper at the Harbor View was hosted by William E. Marchant, one of the hotel's original stockholders and owner of the dry goods store that had furnished the hotel's beddings, linens, and draperies. Marchant's guests that summer night, about forty in all, were members of his Sunday school class and their families.

That July evening, reported the *Vineyard Gazette*, the party "enjoyed the appointments of this charming hotel for an hour, Manager Drew personally looking after the comfort and setting at ease each and every guest, by giving them the freedom of the house."

The Harbor View lobby and stairway to guest rooms above.

During the evening, piano solos by Miss Dunham and Rev. Mr. Scripps, a duet by Misses Huxford and Norton, a reading by Miss Dunham, and a recitation by Miss Norton were rendered, much to the enjoyment of the party of the evening, as well as to the permanent guests of the house.

One week later came the grand opening banquet. The hotel had sent out some four hundred invitations for its opening celebration on July 23, and hundreds attended on a beautiful moonlit night.

Entertainment was provided by the popular singer Mattie Josephine Atkins of Boston and Denver; the hotel's broad piazzas were hung with Chinese lanterns, the parlors decorated and ablaze with light. Dancing continued late into the night to the music of a string quartet from a band, and cake and ice cream were served. The *Vineyard Gazette* reported breathlessly on the costumes of the ladies in attendance: Chinese silk and diamonds, chiffon and satin, lace and pearls.

The hundreds who availed themselves of the Harbor View's invitation that Thursday evening, reported the *Vineyard Gazette*, "can testify to the cordial greeting and princely hospitality of the receiving, fully in line with the high reputation which the Harbor View, in a few short weeks, has deservedly gained."

MIZPAH OR HARBOR VIEW?

NAMES CONSIDERED FOR THE HOTEL IN 1891

Hotel Mizpah, Harbor View, Hotel Nashaquitsa,
Hotel Edgarton, The Montezuma, The Swasey,
Hotel Nunpaug & Hotel Quinomica

What is in a name? Pretty much everything, according to the 800 people who tried to name the new hotel.

The *Vineyard Gazette* on November 21, 1890, launched a competition asking the public to send it suitable names for the new hotel. The prize was to be a copy of Webster's International Dictionary, just published by G. & C. Merriam & Co., Springfield, Massachusetts, which retailed for $12 and was described by the newspaper as "by far the most elegant unabridged Dictionary ever published."

Six hundred votes poured in by mid-December, with "Hotel Edgartown" taking a commanding early lead and "Harbor View" a distant sixth behind such colorful names as "Hotel Mizpah," "Hotel Nashaquitsa," and even a deliberate misspelling, "Hotel Edgarton."

Then came a stream of letters to the editor. Correspondents protested that some ballot stuffers cared more about winning the dictionary than giving Edgartown's new landmark a fitting name. These sentiments resonated in town. By the end of January, "Harbor View" had inched into the lead with 114 votes, "Hotel Edgartown" close behind with 100.

When the voting closed in February with more than 800 ballots cast, "Harbor View" was the winner, and L. C. Bliss of Cambridge was awarded the dictionary. Bliss wrote, "Nature has given Edgartown one of the most picturesque harbors on our coast, which only needs to be known to be appreciated. A good picture of the hotel, to hang up in public places and on steamers, would be a judicious way to advertise; and the very name, Harbor View, would make prominent just what we all know will be the great attraction—the water."

The long list of colorful suggestions—The Montezuma, The Swasey, Hotel Nunpaug, Hotel Quinomica, and all the others—was set aside. In the end, the people of Edgartown understood that their new hotel's greatest asset was the harbor it looked out upon.

800

NUMBER OF EDGARTOWN
RESIDENTS WHO VOTED
TO SELECT THE NAME
OF THE NEW HOTEL.

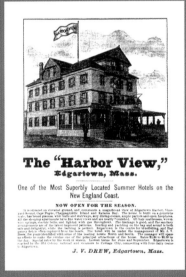

*This newspaper ad announced
the hotel's opening.*

1892
- TO -
1902

When it was built, the Harbor View sat at the start of Starbuck Neck, a then empty stretch of land.

SEVENTY-EIGHT DAYS

1892–1902

*It wasn't much time to make a profit, but the hotel had,
in fact, never been about profit—more about civic revival.
At that, it seemed to excel.*

If the first year for the Harbor View had been a roaring success, the first dozen years were more like a sea voyage—sometimes smooth, sometimes rough, always interesting.

During those first twelve years, the Harbor View had more than doubled in size, cemented its place at the hub of seasonal life of Edgartown, and went through its first bankruptcy. It was owned for an hour by an arsonist, saw its first two managers come and go, and hosted a celebration that ended the town's estrangement with the thriving resort of Cottage City (now Oak Bluffs) that had bested Edgartown for years as a place to vacation.

It was an eventful start for the new grand dame of North Water Street. But it certainly wasn't easy.

In the summer of 1892, a year after it opened, the Harbor View's owners hired W. D. Carpenter as manager, who left his position as manager of the failing lodge at Mattakeset that so many had hoped would help revive Edgartown. The new hotel's guest register was full that season, but the season was over in seventy-eight days, and the expenses of launching the enterprise had been heavy.

A parade of creditors—from carpenters and sellers of furnishings to suppliers of food for the dining room tables—filed liens against the hotel at the county courthouse for bills unpaid. The Harbor View's rates of $2.50 to $3.50 by the day ("Lowest rates for June and September!") simply didn't cover the startup costs.

A view to the Harbor View from the popular bathing beach on Chappaquiddick.

In December 1892 a small notice appeared in the newspaper: Walker, Townsend, and Mayhew, the three owners of the Edgartown Hotel Company, had defaulted on their mortgage, and the Harbor View Hotel was slated for a public auction and sale.

The hotel seemed to have failed almost before it had even gotten started.

Yet when the foreclosure auction was held in April 1893, a remarkable pair of transactions took place. First, Augustus G. Wesley, owner of the Wesley House hotel in Cottage City, purchased the property with a high bid of $6,600. He immediately sold the property back to Walker,

Townsend, and Mayhew for the sum of "one dollar and other considerations."

The three owners of the Harbor View had clearly refinanced their business, leaving the creditors to fight over the $6,600 but writing off the early costs of building and promoting the hotel—while, most importantly, keeping the Harbor View alive.

Wesley, who had obviously been the owners' agent in the foreclosure auction, became notorious in Island history the next year when he was convicted and served time in the Edgartown jail for attempting to torch his own Wesley House after insuring it against fire for $14,000.

FROM FAIRY SHIPS TO LECTURES

It was almost as if it had always been there.

By the summer of 1893 Edgartown was beginning to get the hang of summer resort life—and the Harbor View was at the center of seasonal activity. The hotel hosted public dances, patriotic services on Independence Day, a show of fire balloons on July 14, musical entertainments in its parlor, and an illustrated lecture, *The Life of Columbus*. Tennis tournaments were played on the hotel's new courts, and baseball games on its field. The hotel and town jointly sponsored foot races on Main Street and a tub race at the bathing beach.

Tennis courts on the hotel lawn

Foot races on Main Street, Edgartown, in the summer of 1893.

Although the season was less than three months long, the Harbor View and the town intended to make use of every minute.

Taking advantage of its beautiful harbor as a venue, the town launched the Edgartown Boat Parade that summer, its own version of the famous Illumination Night that Cottage City had started in 1869. Town leaders organized a parade of two dozen decorated and illuminated sailboats on the night of August 11. Fireworks were shot into the sky as sailboats rounded a marker off the lighthouse in front of the Harbor View, parading for the judges on the steamboat wharf. Citizens watched from the wharves, the lighthouse bridge, and the deck of the revenue cutter USS *Dexter* at its North Wharf mooring. The first prize, a beautiful silk pennant bearing the letters EBP for the Edgartown Boat Parade, was awarded to William W. King of Edgartown, who had decorated his sailboat to give the appearance of a miniature "fairy ship."

THE WEEK OF TENNIS MATCHES THAT AUGUST AT THE HARBOR VIEW'S COURTS WAS SPIRITED— PERHAPS A BIT TOO SPIRITED, IN FACT, AS MAY BE DEDUCED FROM THE *VINEYARD GAZETTE*'S STUDIOUSLY G-RATED ACCOUNT:

"For certain reasons we forbear criticizing the conduct of one of the players, hoping that the next time he takes part in a tournament at Edgartown he will be wiser in the use of 'the unruly member.' The umpires rendered their decisions with courteous firmness and to the satisfaction of all fair-minded, disinterested persons, and if some of the lookers-on had been as ready to abide by their decisions as were the players with one exception, it would have added much to the pleasure of the games."

SUMMER WORK

In January 1894 the Harbor View's owners hired F. A. Douglas as the hotel's new manager. Douglas, superintendent of schools in the town of Winthrop, Massachusetts, was the first in a long line of educators to find the Harbor View's season a perfect fit for summer employment. Douglas was already a seasoned hotel manager but looking for new work. The Highland House in Cottage City, which he had managed for three years, was destroyed by fire in October 1893.

Rockers and throw rugs in the hotel lobby.

As an educator in Winthrop for thirty-seven years, Douglas proved himself a man of energy and administrative skill. He began his career as principal in 1890 when Winthrop's entire school system comprised eleven classrooms, a staff of twelve teachers, and a graduating high school class of eight. When he retired as superintendent in 1927, the district's enrollment was more than three thousand students; four graduates of Harvard University that year (three of them cum laude) were alumni of the Winthrop schools; and every school building then serving the district had been constructed on Douglas's watch.

Each summer, Douglas brought the same competence and energy to his job at the Harbor View. Reporting on a week of lively activity at the hotel in July of his first summer—"an enjoyable hop" and a night of progressive euchre with eight tables in play—the *Vineyard Gazette* declared, "Mr. and Mrs. Douglas, of the Harbor View, are unceasing in their attention to the comfort and entertainment of guests, and the house is deservedly enjoying its most prosperous season."

With Douglas again in charge, the Harbor View's next season in 1895 opened on June 20 and closed on September 5. From start to finish, seventy-eight days was a frighteningly short window in which to keep a business viable. And yet the hotel's owners and new manager pressed ahead with ambitious plans for expansion.

For the summer of 1896, a dining room seating 120 persons—twice the former capacity—was added on the northeast side of the Harbor View. The former dining room was

"A week at the Harbor View is said to be one long day of comfort and content."

VINEYARD GAZETTE

The Harbor View dining room was expanded to seat 120 in the summer of 1896.

remodeled as a ladies' writing and reading room, and piazzas were extended around the new addition. John L. Mayhew, one of the owners, was in charge of the work, supervising a force of carpenters who had come from Cottage City.

The Harbor View's halls, piazzas, and grounds were filled with life each evening, as its hundred and more guests whiled away the summer hours—some with games of whist and euchre, some with social chat. Elderly gentlemen enjoyed their Havana cigars, discussing the outlook for war with Spain as the Cuban push for independence gained momentum; the strains of dancing music called the younger set to the enlarged dining room to trip the light fantastic.

Racing sailboats ply the waters of Edgartown harbor in this aerial view taken sometime after 1938, when the new lighthouse was installed.

ESTRANGED AND REUNITED

After years of watching the summer resort at Cottage City with envy and even resentment, the people of Edgartown sensed a new beginning in 1896. Plans were made for a grand celebration—what they hoped would be the most brilliant event of the season, and perhaps in Edgartown's history as a summer resort. The guests of honor at a program of events on August 19 were to be the Board of Trade from Cottage City, whose success as a resort Edgartown had envied for so many years.

On the appointed day, a fleet of wheelmen led by Professor A. B. Guilford of Jersey City paraded through the streets on brightly decorated bicycles to meet a trainload of business leaders from Cottage City. Accompanied by the Vineyard Zouaves, a uniformed marching company, and the twenty-two-piece Pawtucket City Band, the visitors marched through town down Main Street, then up the length of North Water Street to the Harbor View. Porches all along the route were decorated for the occasion, and townspeople lined the streets to applaud the visitors and band.

With their distinguished guests watching from the Harbor View's porches, the Zouaves performed precision French Algerian marching drills on the tennis courts beside the east veranda. An illuminated boat parade sailed through the harbor at 9 p.m., serenaded by musicians from the deck of the schooner *Glide*, festooned with lanterns and anchored at Osborn's Wharf. The first prize, an elegant gold medal, was awarded to John E. White, who had decorated his sailboat as a windmill. At 10 p.m. the visitors sat down for a banquet with many toasts and speeches, which lasted until well after midnight.

"WHAT IS THE 19TH OF AUGUST
IN THIS TOWN ANYWAY?"

An amazed visitor remarked as the festivities played out in Edgartown.

At night, the hotel is a striking sight, reflecting in the pond in front of it.

In the wee hours of Thursday morning, the foot parade of Oak Bluffs notables and their Edgartown hosts marched back to the train station for their trip home, the band breaking into "Marching through Georgia" as the entourage reached the terminal. The sense was general that this had been a moment of reconciliation between two towns so torn by schism in 1880.

Declared the *Vineyard Gazette*, "Each and all expressed the wish that the affection which has been restored between the old mother town and her beautiful daughter located on the northern border may grow with each succeeding year. May many other similar occasions follow in the years to come!"

GROWTH AND EXPANSION

By the summer of 1897, new enterprises were springing up across Edgartown to serve the influx of summer people. For entertainment, hotel guests could walk to the foot of Main Street and visit Edgartown's new Whaling Museum, presided over by a genuine—and presumably salty—former sea captain.

Edgartown was connected to Woods Hole and New Bedford (and its trains to all points) by daily ferry service that began on June 21, the first day of summer. Excursionists to town were greeted with advertising cards headlined "Information Regarding Edgartown" and featuring a bird's-eye sketch of the village.

The Harbor View, freshly repainted, opened on June 24. In July, manager Douglas became both owner and proprietor, purchasing the business from Mayhew, Townsend, and Walker. Douglas, seeing a demand for summer rooms that was outstripping supply, quickly made plans for expansion. In August he announced that work would begin after Labor Day on a thirty-eight-room annex just east of the main building, connected to the hotel by verandas.

"On every hand we hear enthusiastic comments on the fine appearance which the new addition to the Harbor View is taking on," reported the *Vineyard Gazette*. "This enlarged hotel, which will contain some eighty lodging rooms, will be an important factor in the future growth of Edgartown as a summer resort, as the original house has been in the past."

Once again, crews employed by John Mayhew were put to work plumbing the new annex. But when Douglas reached out for capital to support his ambitious expansion project, Mayhew was not involved. In April 1898, with the season

HARBOR VIEW GUESTS THAT SUMMER COULD EAT IN THE HOTEL DINING ROOM OR VISIT THE BONAIR CAFÉ, SERVING FULL DINNERS FOR

———— *Price* ————

80 ¢

with a choice of four pies for dessert: cream, squash, custard, or apple.

Below: F. A. Douglas, manager, prepared this early promotional brochure for the hotel in 1896.

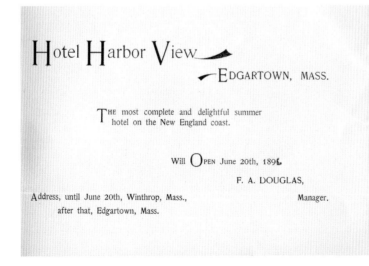

A BELLE PERFORMS

Guests of the Harbor View sponsored
programs at the town hall, including
a performance by Belle Boyd, the
Celebrated Rebel Spy.

Belle was a former West Virginia
debutante who had charmed her town's
occupying Union officers into revealing
battle plans, did two stints in prison,
and then spent her later years on tour,
presenting dramatic accounts of
her Civil War experiences.

"I HAVE NEVER HEARD
HER EQUAL; UNDOUBTEDLY
THE BEST AND MOST
ENJOYABLE ENTERTAINMENT
I EVER ATTENDED."

Captain S. L. Norton

approaching, Walker and Townsend bought back into the Harbor View. This new partnership—each man, along with Douglas, owning a third of the enterprise— would lead the hotel through its next ten years.

In these early days of tourism, just as now, investors in the resort industry understood that the Vineyard, though a place apart, depends on the national economy for a supply of people who feel safe spending money on their vacations. War seemed inevitable after the sinking of the American warship, USS *Maine*, in Havana Harbor in February 1898, and this event had thrown a cloud over the coming season. But reporting on the sale of the Harbor View, the *Vineyard Gazette* wrote, "It is apparent that these gentlemen are satisfied that a war with Spain will not seriously curtail the number of visitors to our town the present season, and we are told the outlook for a successful business at the hotel is good."

The new owners were not disappointed in their investment. Guests were registering weekly at the hotel from across Massachusetts, New York, New Jersey, and Washington, DC—about a hundred in residence at a time. Plans were announced in January 1899 for a new kitchen at the back of the Harbor View to accommodate all the dining guests. It was completed in time for that summer.

BUYING MORE LAND AND COTTAGES

The Harbor View began the twentieth century as it had ended the nineteenth —with another ambitious round of expansion. In February, local contractor William G. Manter was hired to construct a second annex, this one west of the main hotel, with two billiard rooms, a smoking room, and bowling alley on the main floor, and five good-sized lodging rooms above. The addition opened on August 1, at the midpoint of the hotel's summer season.

With this building project, the hotel's owners nearly filled the envelope of their property on the bluffs of Starbuck Neck. In July 1900, Walker, Townsend, and Douglas purchased nine acres adjoining the hotel property from the estate of Captain Henry Holt. This land enabled the Harbor View's owners to continue their program of buying some of Edgartown's grandest houses and relocating them to the hotel property, where they were restored and offered for summer enjoyment "for parties desiring the seclusion and quiet of cottage life."

One of the most notable acquisitions was the Huxford House, which was moved to the hotel grounds from next door to the Old Whaling Church, in the lot between the church and another Edgartown landmark, the Dr. Daniel Fisher House.

IN AN ATTEMPT TO DUPLICATE THE SUCCESS OF THE COTTAGES OF THE RIGHTLY NAMED "COTTAGE CITY," THE HARBOR VIEW BEGAN MOVING OLD HOUSES TO ITS GROUNDS TO PROVIDE A BIT OF COTTAGE LIFE. THE COTTAGES ARE NOW A POPULAR PART OF THE HARBOR VIEW.

The modern cottages face a green square that is popular both for children to play and for tents for special events.

The Huxford House was formally dedicated as an annex to the hotel at the end of July 1900. The house was entirely renovated, plumbed, and nicely furnished, providing fourteen additional rooms for the Harbor View. It was connected with the main hotel by a plank walk illumined at night by streetlamps.

So successful were the Huxford House and the Harbor View's original cottage that plans were made to construct two more as hotel annexes over the winter of 1900–1901. With its cottages and annexes, the Harbor View had grown in its first decade to become the largest and grandest resort hotel on Martha's Vineyard.

HOTEL
& LIBRARY

THE EDGARTOWN LIBRARY BUDGET IN 1897 WAS

Less Than

$150

This page from the minutes of the Edgartown Library trustees records a gift to the library from guests of the Harbor View.

For most of their history, the Harbor View Hotel and the Edgartown Free Public Library have been bookends along North Water Street's grand stretch of captains' houses. The library opened in a rented room on Main Street on June 11, 1891, just three weeks before the Harbor View welcomed its first guests. In 1904 the library got its own building, a gift to the town from steel magnate Andrew Carnegie, on a lot donated by Caroline Warren at the western end of North Water Street.

Myra Walker, the young wife of hotel owner Dr. Thomas J. Walker, was a library trustee for more than two decades, and she encouraged her husband and the guests of the Harbor View to make the library one of their charities.

In 1897 the Harbor View collected donations from its guests, which were presented to the library trustees by Edgartown's noted summer celebrity, Sol Smith Russell, at the end of the summer. The gift of $35—a huge boost for the library, whose annual budget was less than $150—permitted the purchase of so many books that the library immediately began seeking larger quarters.

Other summer visitors contributed to the library by placing a one- or two-dollar bill in their borrowed books when they left for the season.

With the gift of $4,000 from steel magnate Andrew Carnegie and of land from a resident who loved libraries, Caroline Osborne Warren, Edgartown built its first public library at 58 North Water Street in 1904.

1902
– TO –
1948

By the time this picture was taken in 1902, development on the harbor had begun to reach the Harbor View.

A BENEFIT TO EDGARTOWN

1902–1948

The new century brought new visitors as word of Edgartown spread, and new investments, both in the hotel and in the surrounding village.

The early years of the twentieth century were heady ones for Edgartown, and the town and its visitors were getting into the rhythms of a new century. Automobiles, though not yet common in 1905, were no longer a rarity meriting headlines in the local paper. Even so, Elmer Bliss, owner of the Regal Shoe Company who had a nationwide chain of stores, made headlines and history in 1900 when he brought his Locomobile down from Boston.

Streets were still surfaced with scallop shells, but one of Edgartown's municipal services was now the regular wetting-down of streets by a horse-drawn water tanker, to make driving on them easier. Capitalizing on the tourists strolling the streets that summer, the steamer *Martha's*

Vineyard offered regular excursions from the Edgartown wharf to Gay Head, fare 50 cents.

On a typical week in late July 1905, the listings of fresh arrivals at the Harbor View included guests from across Massachusetts, Rhode Island, Connecticut, New York, New Jersey, New Hampshire, Virginia, Illinois, Iowa, Michigan, and Missouri. Clearly, news of Edgartown and its premier hotel had reached far beyond the Vineyard.

Inside, the Harbor View had in 1902 added new dormitory rooms for hotel staff onto a new kitchen wing, the hotel lobby and dining room had been expanded, and the new office received a handsome stone fireplace. New seasonal owners were investing money in the classic old

captains' houses of North Water Street that had previously been almost derelict, and new summer homes were springing up on the land around the Harbor View that had been purchased by a farsighted developer and subdivided in 1897, adding to the feeling of prosperity emerging around the hotel.

The Harbor View Hotel and its town were both thriving, but Frank Douglas, the hotel's hardworking manager since 1894 and part-time owner since 1897, decided that after ten years it was time to make room for some vacations of his own. He kept his winter job as superintendent of schools in Winthrop for two more decades, but in April 1908 he sold his interest in the hotel back to his partners, Townsend and Walker, and sailed for a summer in Europe with his family. Wrote the *Vineyard Gazette*, "He and his efficient wife will be greatly missed among us, and we wish them a happy and successful future."

Henry W. Morse, an experienced hotel man from Boston, became the Harbor View's fourth manager. He had been the manager for several years of the Winneegan, a resort hotel on Baker's Island, five miles offshore from the town of Salem. That hotel, built in 1887 and bearing an uncanny resemblance to the Harbor View, had burned to the ground in the spring of 1906.

The Winneegan Hotel on Baker's Island, lost to fire in 1906, and where the Harbor View's new manager had learned his trade.

Soon after Douglas sold his share back to his partners, Walker filed a "caveat" at the Dukes County Courthouse, a formal document warning anyone interested in the property that a dispute had arisen between himself and Townsend, throwing a cloud over the property's title. In November 1909 Walker bought out Townsend, becoming the Harbor View's sole owner.

In the fall of 1910 Walker purchased the derelict Mattakeset Lodge at the end of the long-dormant railway line at Katama, hiring his son Raymond as foreman to oversee its dismantling for lumber to use at the Harbor View

BUSINESS WAS BOOMING, AND THE RIPPLES WERE FELT THROUGHOUT
EDGARTOWN, WHERE THE STEEP POPULATION DECLINE HAD BEEN
ARRESTED—LEAVING THE COUNT OF 1,156 FROM 1890, THE YEAR THE
HARBOR VIEW PROJECT WAS ANNOUNCED, AS THE HISTORIC LOW EBB.

With the hotel as the backdrop, visitors and townspeople watch the fireworks on July 4.

property. Contractor George S. Norton was hired to move, overland with heavy tackle, the south end of the old lodge from Katama to the Harbor View campus, where it was set up as a summer cottage.

The tedious two-mile trip, which took several months, was followed closely by townspeople. Reported the *Vineyard Gazette* on March 23, 1911, "The building today is at a point on Pease's Point Way, about midway between the North Schoolhouse and the residence of James E. Chadwick." Another section of the lodge was transported into town and still stands today as the offices of the Martha's Vineyard Land Bank.

By the summer of 1911, everyone in town was calling the hotel "Dr. Walker's Harbor View."

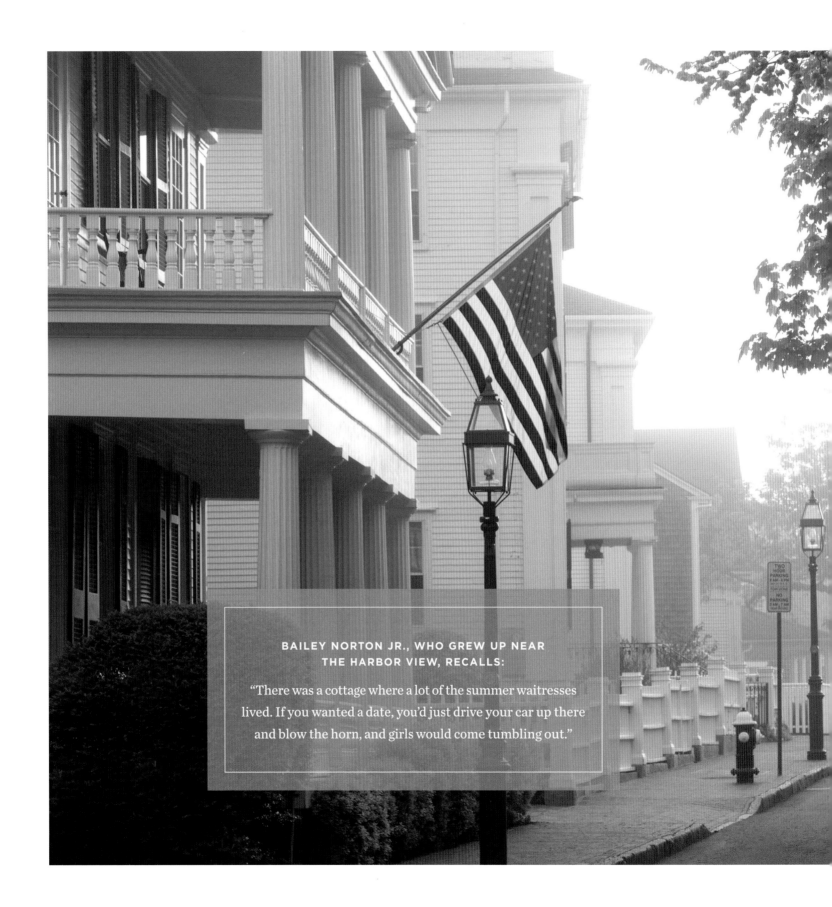

**BAILEY NORTON JR., WHO GREW UP NEAR
THE HARBOR VIEW, RECALLS:**

"There was a cottage where a lot of the summer waitresses
lived. If you wanted a date, you'd just drive your car up there
and blow the horn, and girls would come tumbling out."

VOICES

The Harbor View as Playground

S. Bailey Norton Jr., born in November 1920 and brought up in The Anchors—the childhood home that now serves the town council on aging—is a living repository of Edgartown history. As a boy growing up on the streets of Edgartown, Norton says, he saw the Harbor View as the center of activity for a strange and separate breed of people—the summer crowd:

"EVERYONE SEEMED TO GET DRESSED UP EVEN IF THEY WERE JUST GOING TO THE BATHING BEACH FOR THE DAY—JACKET AND TIE, PANAMA HAT. I REMEMBER THEM WALKING BACK AND FORTH INTO TOWN FROM THE HARBOR VIEW. IN THOSE DAYS, WE LOCALS WOULD STICK TO THE WATER SIDE OF THE STREET, AND THE LAND SIDE OF NORTH WATER STREET SEEMED TO BE RESERVED FOR THE SUMMER PEOPLE. WE'D STAY ON OUR OWN SIDE OF THE STREET."

Every summer after Labor Day, when the Harbor View closed, the hotel grounds became a favorite haunt for the boys of town, with the hotel itself their jungle gym. "On Saturdays and Sundays in the off-season there wouldn't be much around for kids to do. Behind the Harbor View property on Fuller Street was an open field where the boys used to play scrub baseball and kick the can. Some days we'd go out and crawl over the fire escapes of the Harbor View. We'd play follow-the-leader, seeing who could climb the farthest up one roof or jump to another. It was our playground."

Dr. Walker's pharmacy on North Water Street was downstairs from the family's residence, in the building that is now Murdick's Fudge.

DR. WALKER TAKES CHARGE

Thomas J. Walker was born in Ontario, Canada, in 1845, into a family of seven sons and four daughters whose ancestors hailed from County Tyrone in Northern Ireland. After graduating from medical school at the University of Vermont and receiving his hospital training in Hartford, Connecticut, he came to Martha's Vineyard in 1873 for what was intended as a three-month stay—to recuperate after a bout with tuberculosis at the home of a medical school classmate, Dr. Orlin Mayhew of Vineyard Haven. Walker stayed, joining the practice of Dr. William Luce of West Tisbury, marrying the doctor's daughter Hepzibah, and opening his own practice in Edgartown five years later.

Skilled both as a physician and a businessman, Walker quickly took a place at the center of the town's commercial life. A man most comfortable when he was in charge,

Walker was an owner and director of the Edgartown Water Company, a director of the Edgartown National Bank, and proprietor of his own shop, the Edgartown Drug Store.

Fond of new technologies and quick to adopt them, Walker installed the town's first telegraph service in his shop in 1903 and had every room of the Harbor View Hotel wired with telephones in 1911. He was one of the first Edgartown residents to install a then-new form of carbide gas lighting at his drugstore and home, but he abandoned it after an explosion in December 1902 blew out all the shop's windows and bumped one side of the building completely off its foundation.

Walker was proud of his handsome traveling rig, the team of horses and the buggy he rode to Gay Head and back to call on patients Up-Island. And when the automobile appeared, he embraced it enthusiastically. The account of personal property in his estate included four Buicks and a Ford.

Driving this team, Dr. Walker called on patients as far away as Gay Head.

Hepsie Walker died of tuberculosis in 1884, and the next year Walker married Myra Marchant, the daughter of Cornelius Marchant of Edgartown. Myra was an avid photographer, and the Edgartown Drug Store sold postcards printed in Germany with her images of Island scenes. Their son, Raymond, was born in 1886; their daughter, Lucretia, was born in 1893, the year the new Harbor View Hotel went through foreclosure.

Lucretia's daughter, Eileen Walker Robinson—now a resident of the campgrounds in Oak Bluffs—says no one in the family remembers ever hearing Myra, who was some twenty years younger than her husband, call him anything but "Dr. Walker." ("What she called him when they were alone together," she adds, "of course nobody knows.")

Walker spent long nights at Island bedsides during the flu pandemic of 1918, which killed more than 650,000 people in America, and it was in the midst of this experience that he prepared his last will and testament.

PASSING THE TORCH—BUT NOT EASILY

Walker may have been prepared to consider his own mortality, but not to give up the control over his enterprises that had been the hallmark of an entrepreneurial, take-charge life.

In his will, Walker named Andrew Church Littlefield, a fellow director of the Edgartown National Bank, as trustee over his estate. Establishing a testamentary trust is a common enough way to protect an estate until minor children reach adulthood. But Thomas Walker took this to an extreme—authorizing Littlefield to distribute income to the children, but denying them any access to only half the estate itself until they reached the age of fifty, and the final half at age sixty.

This controlling gesture would reach across the decades to shape the fortunes of Walker's family and of the Harbor View Hotel. At Walker's death in May 1920, his son was 34 years old and his daughter 27—and the average life expectancy in the United States was just 53.6 years.

Perhaps realizing that such an unusual document as his last will needed iron-clad verification, Walker arranged for three witnesses: Edgartown National Bank founder Julian W. Vose; the legendary catboat builder Manuel Swartz, whose workshop is now Edgartown's Old Sculpin Gallery; and Sarah M. Norton, a daughter of the noted Edgartown whaling captain, Ichabod Norton, and Walker's bookkeeper for many years.

If Walker had doubts about his own children, it was clear he had none about Littlefield: the somber, conservative man would be running the hotel for a long time—and running it straight down.

AT HIS DEATH, DR. WALKER ENTRUSTED THE HOTEL NOT TO A VISIONARY BUT TO A MAN OF CONSERVATIVE FINANCIAL INSTINCTS AND LITTLE THOUGHT ABOUT IMPROVEMENT.

Copyright 1905 by the Rotograph Co.
A 6885 North Water St., Edgartown, Mass.

North Water Street in 1905, with its single sidewalk—reserved by tradition for summer people.

RUNNING HARBOR VIEW INTO THE GROUND

Andrew Littlefield, trustee of the Walker family estate, was not what anyone would call a taker of risks. A slender man of probity and conservative financial instincts, he was born in Edgartown in 1873—Walker's junior by twenty-eight years—the son of Captain Aaron D. Littlefield of the U.S. Revenue Cutter Service, and his wife, Betsey W. B. Stuart.

Littlefield and his wife, Charlotte, were childless. They resided in Boston for many years but maintained a close association with Edgartown, moving permanently to their house on School Street in the early 1930s. He served as a director and vice president of the Edgartown National Bank, as a library trustee, and for several years on the Edgartown finance committee. In his working life, he traveled for many years as a salesman of decorative woven fabrics. Charlotte was the organist at the Federated Church.

> ## *"Andrew was so conservative he wouldn't pay a dime to see the Statue of Liberty pee."*
>
> BOB CARROLL
> *Future owner of the Harbor View*

Littlefield was a scrupulous manager of assets, not a visionary. And on his twenty-nine-year watch as steward of the Harbor View, says Walker's granddaughter, Eileen Walker Robinson, "He ran the place into the ground. He watched it pretty carefully, but he didn't put anything into it."

Among the Harbor View's many stewards over its history, Littlefield is notable as the only one who did not put his personal stamp on the place with some major improvement or expansion. The Littlefield era, for the hotel, was a time not of change or new initiatives, but of going through the motions for nearly three decades.

Walker's son, Raymond, had helped his father with maintenance of the Harbor View, including the dismantling of the

The original Harbor View building at left, with its annex.

old Mattakeset Lodge for use at the Walker hotel property. Young Raymond married the local Barbara Coffin and raised a daughter and two sons—one of whom, Thomas Jackson Walker, rose to the rank of vice admiral in the U.S. Navy.

Raymond Walker entertained dreams of following in his father's footsteps and managing the Harbor View. "He went to Dartmouth and studied business there," says Eileen Walker Robinson, "and he came back with the intention of running the hotel." But then a family tragedy intervened.

"Eileen Walker Killed in Coasting Accident," declared the front-page headline in the *Vineyard Gazette* of March 3, 1929. The vivacious seventeen-year-old daughter of Raymond and Barbara Walker had been killed instantly, together with a fellow student at Wheaton College, when their bobsled jumped the track on a winter outing at Poland Spring, Maine, and careened into a tree.

Her family was devastated, recalls Eileen Walker Robinson (named by her mother for the sledding victim). Unable to face the snows of New England winter, which reminded them of their loss, the Walkers moved to Daytona, Florida, not returning to Edgartown until decades later, when Raymond was in his final years of failing health.

So it fell to Andrew Littlefield to usher the Harbor View across the years that spanned the Depression and the Second World War—not a time of booming tourist trade for the Island of Martha's Vineyard.

"THE VINEYARD IS, IN TRUTH, ONE OF THE LEAST EXPENSIVE SUMMER RESORTS.
A VACATION HERE IS NOT AN EXTRAVAGANCE. . . . THIS IS A YEAR TO COME,
NOT A YEAR TO STAY AWAY."

Vineyard Gazette

"ONE OF THE LEAST EXPENSIVE RESORTS"

The 1930s were a decade when the resort industry on Martha's Vineyard didn't so much expand as merely hang on. New construction on the Island came nearly to a halt during the Great Depression, as it did across the nation. Some Island contractors went bankrupt, and their laborers went back to ocean fishing, the Vineyard's traditional livelihood of last resort. The *Vineyard Gazette* tried to put a happy face on the situation, launching a special spring paper promoting the Island, the Invitation Edition, and writing in 1931, "The Vineyard is, in truth, one of the least expensive summer resorts. A vacation here is not an extravagance. . . . This is a year to come, not a year to stay away."

One of the government's Depression-era projects, the Civilian Conservation Corps, set up a camp in the Vineyard's state forest, employing hundreds of men to clear fire lanes and make roads, but that did little to boost the Island economy. It took World War II to end the Depression years—and introduce thousands of American soldiers to the charms of Martha's Vineyard while stationed here for aerial training and staged amphibious assaults.

In 1939, Littlefield won the court's permission to create a new corporation, Harbor View Hotel Inc., with Raymond and Lucretia Walker as the shareholders, to begin the process of transferring full ownership of Dr. Walker's estate to them. Lucretia was forty-six years old, but Raymond was fifty-three, and the court decided that this arrangement honored the remarkable will of their father closely enough.

After the war years, the seasonal life of Martha's Vineyard began returning to its familiar rhythms, but Littlefield was in no position to open a new chapter for the Harbor View. A medical crisis in November 1944 had resulted in an eight-week hospitalization in Boston; his obituary ten years later was discreet about the details, noting only, "In 1944 Mr. Littlefield underwent a major operation from which he made a good recovery but without regaining his former physique."

It would fall to one of Edgartown's most enterprising men to lead the fifteen-year effort that lifted the Harbor View from its doldrums and reestablished it as the grand dame of Island resort hotels. His name was Alfred Hall.

— *That* —
Summer of '46
Shirley Mayhew

SHIRLEY MAYHEW, WHO LIVES IN WEST TISBURY, WORKED AS A HARBOR VIEW WAITRESS IN 1946, DURING THE SUMMER BETWEEN HER SOPHOMORE AND JUNIOR YEARS AT BROWN UNIVERSITY. "IN THOSE DAYS," SHE SAYS, "ELDERLY PEOPLE AND FAMILIES CAME TO THE HARBOR VIEW FOR A MONTH OR THE WHOLE SEASON. I REMEMBER THEY HAD A HUGE ROPE HANGING IN EVERY BEDROOM WITH A KNOT EVERY FOOT OR SO, AND A SIGN SAYING, 'IN CASE OF FIRE, THROW OUT AND CLIMB DOWN.' I MEAN, THIS WAS AN OLD WOOD BUILDING WITH ALL THESE ELDERLY PEOPLE STAYING THERE. I THOUGHT, 'OH MY GOD, I HOPE THERE'S NO FIRE HERE THIS SUMMER.'"

The big event of the season, as Mayhew recalls it, was a brief but effective strike by the waitresses.

"We were getting

$30 PER MONTH

plus our room and board, and the food was no good. We had a meeting with our manager, and we told him we were unhappy with the food we were getting. String beans three nights in a row, no eggs for breakfast—I think we even told him that if we don't get better food, we're going to strike. He didn't believe us. So the next day, we just didn't show up to serve lunch. The busboys told us that all these elderly people were milling around in the kitchen, looking for something to eat. The next day, our food was greatly improved."

— 1902 —

The Edgartown Lighthouse we know was preceded by an actual house, on the beach in front of the Harbor View Hotel, with the keeper and his family inside and the light on the rooftop. It was originally built in 1828, and the first keeper had to row to work, since there was no pier connecting the lighthouse to the shore.

The popular story of the current lighthouse is that it was replaced by the Coast Guard in 1939 after being damaged in the hurricane of 1938. This is true, but it's not the whole story.

The Coast Guard in those days was replacing its manned lighthouses along the East Coast with simple automated lights atop decidedly unromantic skeletons of galvanized steel, and Edgartown had been loudly protest-ing the agency's announcement that its lighthouse was costly and inefficient and was going to go.

In August 1938 the commissioner of lighthouses agreed to give Edgartown a surplus Coast Guard tower at the inner harbor entrance and to paint it gleaming white.

Edgartown's lobbying had won it a scenic lighthouse, a standard-issue model similar to the tower at East Chop, but the keeper's job was gone, and the Coast Guard also abandoned its upkeep of the wooden walkway from North Water Street to the lighthouse—a popular Edgartown attraction known as the "bridge of sighs."

Reporting this news, the *Vineyard Gazette* predicted that even without care, the bridge was in good enough condition to last at least a decade.

Above: This lighthouse was already slated for replacement by an automated light when the hurricane of 1938 badly damaged it.
Bottom Left: Sand begins to build around the new lighthouse. Bottom Right: A vegetated beach has formed, and the pond's western opening has closed.

— 1952 —   — 2013 —

1948
— TO —
1965

Edgartown and the Harbor View begin to take a more modern look in this photo.

A CHERISHED LANDMARK

1948–1965

"Many summer residents who later built homes in Edgartown first came to the Harbor View."

Noting the Harbor View's splendid location at the harbor entrance, the Vineyard Gazette *reminded its readers of the hotel's historic role in jump-starting the summer resort.*

In the years just after the Second World War, the Harbor View continued to be an important destination for families who gathered here to enjoy their summers together. But the Harbor View was no longer the only resort hotel in town. The Edgartown social columns followed weekly arrivals at the Harbor View in the summer of 1949, but also arrivals at the Colonial Inn, the Harborside Inn, the Charlotte Inn, and the Edgartown Inn.

Edgartown, like its neighbor towns on Martha's Vineyard, was now a village of hotels and inns. The town also had a growing community of seasonal visitors who rented or owned their summer homes. In fact, it's likely that by the end of the 1940s, after three decades of management by the penny-pinching Andrew Littlefield, the Harbor View Hotel had more financial value simply as real estate on the residential market than it had as a money-making business—not unlike today.

"The hotel and the cottages really were in bad shape. Everything was in bad shape," recalls Charlotte Hall, Alfred Hall's daughter, who still lives in Edgartown. "The hotel had been reduced to a sort of boardinghouse; there were these faithful people who came every summer and put up with it."

Yet a group of town leaders had already looked past the sad state of the hotel and decided to do something about it.

Which begs the question: Why organize a group of investors to purchase and save an aging hotel? The answer is that

From the early 1960s, a postcard depicting the good life on the beach overlooking the Harbor View.

BY 1949 THE PEOPLE OF
EDGARTOWN SAW THE
HARBOR VIEW NOT JUST
AS ONE HOTEL AMONG
MANY BUT AS A
CHERISHED LANDMARK.

by 1949, the people of Edgartown saw the Harbor View not just as one hotel among many, but as a cherished landmark.

Announcing the hotel's sale that September, the *Vineyard Gazette*, continuing its long-standing support of the now aging hotel, described the Harbor View as an important influence in Edgartown, "long occupying a place of leadership."

Alfred Hall, the prominent businessman representing a group of purchasers, told the newspaper that he and the new owners planned to modernize it and return it to the "same relationship to Edgartown that it had in its heyday."

The 1949 *Vineyard Gazette* story resonates with echoes of the same community spirit that had welcomed the Harbor View's original investors in 1890 as "a roll of honor." Echoed again was a fierce pride in the enterprise as a community endeavor: "Mr. Hall said that the ownership of the new company will be entirely on the Island or among summer residents. There will, he said, be no mainland interest involved."

UNSTOPPABLE ALFRED HALL

Alfred Hall was a dapper human dynamo, a businessman and philanthropist who for some thirty years, at the peak of his long career, owned nearly one-third of the buildings on Edgartown's Main Street.

Born in 1898 to Benjamin and Bessie Hall—his father was proprietor of Hall's Department Store in Edgartown—he was an athletic boy, a graceful baseball player, and one of the fastest runners in town.

> "HE WON RACES SO CONSISTENTLY, THAT HE WAS FINALLY BARRED FROM COMPETITION TO ALLOW OTHERS A CHANCE."
>
> *Noted the* Vineyard Gazette *in his obituary in 1992*
>
> He won a prize for public speaking at the age of fifteen, earned extra money as a teenager by selling his own vegetables from a pushcart, and (trading on his fleetness of foot) ran telegrams—an essential form of communication in those days—from Dr. Walker's drugstore to their recipients across town.

Educated at the University of New Hampshire, Harvard University, and Boston University—his schooling was interrupted by the First World War, where he rose to the rank of captain in the Chemical Warfare Division—he returned to Edgartown in 1923 with a degree in business administration from BU. For a time he worked with his brother Morris in his father's retail store. ("We sold shoes, shirts, socks, sealing wax, and sailing ships," he liked to say in later years.) But Hall's Department Store wasn't big enough to support two families, so Alfred purchased Dr. Worth's drugstore across from the Edgartown National Bank, at the intersection called Four Corners.

Upstairs from the drugstore, in the boom years of the 1920s, Hall operated a seasonal stock brokerage in a room outfitted with plush leather chairs for Edgartown's wealthy summer businessmen, who would lounge and smoke and read the latest ticker-tape prices from a large blackboard. At the end of the season in 1929, as he always did, Alfred Hall closed the brokerage business and cashed in all his stocks—just months before the October market crash that started the Great Depression. Several years later, flush with cash, he purchased the Elm Theatre on Main Street ("475 seats, open three days a week"). Alfred Hall owned and managed five Island movie theaters, including the now closed Strand, Island, and Capawock theaters.

ALFRED HALL
Harbor View Owner

Alfred and Marjorie Hall.

Hall also opened an insurance agency whose business was boosted greatly by the Hurricane of 1938, one of the most powerful ever to hit the New England coast. The storm caused heavy damage across the Vineyard and nearly wiped the fishing village of Menemsha off the map. Prompted, or so he later said, by many people inquiring about places to stay in town, he began to deal in real estate—buying, renovating, renting, and selling homes and commercial properties across Edgartown.

In 1932 he married the love of his life, Marjorie Hayden Lambert, whom he'd first met at the Edgartown Town Hall dances. A young beauty from Brockton, educated in the art schools of Boston, she had summered for years in Edgartown with her aunt, Mattie Lambert Pease. Alfred and Marjorie had three children, Charlotte, Marcia, and Benjamin (all of whom still reside on the Island), and their love of dancing together continued long into their retirement.

Alfred Hall, always a trim and natty figure—he loved his blazers and tweeds, seersucker jackets in summer, and often wearing a bow tie—poured a prodigious amount of energy into civic and philanthropic work on the Island he loved. He was an ardent advocate of regional services, leading the push for the Martha's Vineyard Regional High School and serving as chairman of the regional school committee. He served as president of the Dukes County Historical Society, a director of Martha's Vineyard Community Services, and a trustee of the Martha's Vineyard Hospital, chairing its finance committee.

When Edgartown was faced with the possible demise of the Harbor View Hotel at the close of the 1940s, it was natural that the community should turn to the business leader who was also a leader in the town's civic life.

The Island, one of five movie theatres owned by Alfred Hall.

Beach life in the 1950s.

A FAMILY PROJECT

In December 1949 a new entity, Harbor View Hotel Corp., bought the entire hotel operation from the Walker family's Harbor View Hotel Inc. for $50,000.

Alfred Hall, leader of the purchasing group, was its vice president and managing director. Cornelius S. Lee of New York and Edgartown, founder of the Edgartown Golf Club and a longtime officer of the United States Golf Association, was president of the new company. The board of directors included Edgartown summer residents Roger S. Robinson and John W. Garrett II, and Frank J. Connors, the proprietor of Edgartown's grocery store and meat market. Charles H. Center and his wife, brought in two years earlier, were kept on as managers of the hotel.

Alfred Hall's son, Benjamin Lambert (Buzz) Hall, and his sister Charlotte remember the excitement that surrounded the new project and their father's commitment to it. "The new owners would not go into it unless my father was involved," Buzz recalls.

"He was the one who organized it," says Charlotte. "He said it's a shame for this potential jewel to be falling apart."

Buzz Hall remembers a pattern among the Harbor View clientele of that day: a wealthy woman and her poor relation, staying the summer in the same rooms year after year. Miss Windsor and Miss Wister from Philadelphia were one such pair, he says. Miss Bowen and Miss Blythe were another. Together, the four would play bridge in the card room almost every evening.

The Harbor View needed a thorough freshening up as a destination for a new generation of summer visitors, and Hall set about the task with his characteristic energy. His ally in what became a family project, his children say, was his wife, Marjorie, who had trained in art at the Vesper George School and the Museum School in Boston.

"I remember my mom saying that we have to decorate it with a splash," says Charlotte, "and we have to have a good chef. Those were the two requirements."

It was a time in the Hall family's life when the children were leaving the nest, and Marjorie threw herself wholeheartedly into the renovation. "She loved doing this," recalls Charlotte. "She was a frustrated painter, really, and the Harbor View was her canvas. It was her sense of panache that really helped put the hotel on the map."

For the first years of the 1950s, the Harbor View was a project for the whole Hall family. Charlotte, with her typing skills, did secretarial work in the hotel office. Buzz Hall learned the complexities of the hotel switchboard and dug holes

GETTING THE HARBOR VIEW READY FOR REOPENING UNDER THE HALLS WAS A MAJOR PROJECT.

It involved trips to the venerable F. Schumacher & Co. in New York, founded in 1889 and still in business today, the decorating firm that has helped furnish the White House, the Chambers of the U.S. Supreme Court, and countless distinguished residences. One of the Harbor View cottages was set up as an impromptu spray-paint shop, and most of the hotel's furniture was repainted.

"Mom and Dad were always running back and forth to wholesalers, buying stuff," says Charlotte. "We spruced everything up so it looked neat and airy and summery."

all over the property for the gardener, who replanted the grounds at Mrs. Hall's instructions.

"Mother was the one who planted the first Marissa hydrangeas on the lawns," says Charlotte. "Some of them are still there, along the side, hugging the porch. Everybody has them now. And in the back, she planted a big cutting garden, and with this wonderful gardener they had gladiolas and zinnias and marigolds—everything you could think of for the dining room and the lobby, all summer."

Buzz remembers befriending and being tutored in Latin by the couple who ran the Harbor View's front desk each summer and were teachers in Worcester during the school year. "I paid for the tutoring by taking them out to sail in the harbor," he says. "I'd take them out, and I'd let them take the helm while I read Latin, and they'd correct me."

Owning the Harbor View wasn't all work for the Halls. Buzz and Charlotte Hall have happy memories of family meals served by celebrated chef Henry Haller in the hotel dining room, whom they had recruited after a nationwide search (see story, page 142). Buzz especially remembers the lavish Sunday buffets. "Your appetizer," he recalls, "would be half a lobster."

The dining room, as redecorated by the Halls.

A COMMANDING PRESENCE
ON STARBUCK BLUFF:

By early in the century, the town had begun to
grow up around the Harbor View, but it still
dominated the eastern end of North Water Street.

NEAR DISASTER

The story of the Harbor View Hotel very nearly ended on May 10, 1950, just weeks before it was set to open for its first season under new ownership.

The fire started on that Wednesday afternoon in a second-floor storeroom of the service wing at the back of the building. When Edgartown's volunteer firemen arrived at the scene, flames were pouring from windows and there were concerns that the whole main building and its annex were in danger.

Firemen concentrated on pumping water into the third floor, thinking to flood the fire from above. At first men had trouble getting close to the fire's point of origin because the smoke was so thick. Chief William Silva said later that it was fortunate winds were so low that afternoon. In the early minutes, he considered calling in the Oak Bluffs fire team for help. But a quick change in the color of smoke pouring from the hotel assured him that the fire was coming under control. Two hours after the firefight began, the all-clear signal sounded from the fire horn at the center of town.

An investigation suggested that a carelessly handled cigarette had probably started the blaze. There was concern at first that the smoke and water damage might delay the hotel's opening for the 1950 season, but by week's end it was apparent that the damage was not as bad as first feared, and the opening was not endangered.

In another stroke of good luck, none of the new draperies and venetian blinds prepared by Marjorie Hall for the redecorating effort had yet been put up at the time of the fire.

Buzz and Charlotte Hall say that, as things turned out, the fire of 1950 even had a positive side. "Mother had such wonderful ideas for the hotel—she wanted to make a real splash," recalls Charlotte. "We'd say no, no, we don't have the money for that. But after the fire, when the insurance settlement came, suddenly there was money. They were able to completely redo the dining room."

At a midsummer meeting in that first season of 1950 Alfred Hall told the new ownership group that things were going well. Reported the *Vineyard Gazette*, "A vote of thanks was given him for the time and work he has devoted to the reorganized hotel, an expression of appreciation which was amended to include Mrs. Hall—'She's done a beautiful job of decorating,' Mrs. [Emily] Price Post said." (Post, the famous doyenne of etiquette, had a summer house at 34 Fuller Street in Edgartown that is still noted for its flower gardens.)

Flags fly on North Water Street.

New Managers

In 1956, for the first time, an off-Island group was brought in to take over the Harbor View's management. Treadway Inns, a Boston-based, family-owned company founded in 1912, signed a five-year, renewable contract that November with the Harbor View Hotel Corp.

In an age when national chains were beginning to homogenize the hotel industry across the United States, Treadway Inns was a perfect fit for the Harbor View. No two of the corporation's sixteen properties were alike, and many of them had just the sort of historic resonance that made the Harbor View such a special place.

Hostelries already operated by Treadway included the Sturbridge Inn; the Williamstown Inn; Long Trail Lodge in Rutland, Vermont; and, nearer to home, the Coonamessett Inn in Falmouth. Treadway soon added the Jared Coffin House, a former whaler's mansion on Nantucket, to its portfolio of properties, giving it many old and successful inns throughout New England.

"FOR THE HARBOR VIEW DIRECTORS IT IS SAID THAT BOARD MEMBERS FEEL THEY AND THE STOCKHOLDERS ARE SATISFIED THAT THEY HAVE FULFILLED THEIR PRIMARY PURPOSE: REHABILITATING FOR ITS TRADITIONAL PLACE IN THE TOWN ONE OF ITS FOREMOST AND FIRST CLASS RESORT HOTELS. IN TURNING OVER THE MANAGEMENT TO THE TREADWAY CORPORATION, THE BOARD THEREFORE FEELS IT IS OFFERING TO ITS GUESTS AN ADDED DIMENSION IN FURTHERANCE OF ITS FAITH IN THE TOWN AND ISLAND AND FULFILLMENT OF ITS ORIGINAL PURPOSE."

Vineyard Gazette, *1956*

HARBOR VIEW BROCHURE
Alfred Hall days

ONCE THE HALLS TOOK OVER, THEY WORKED HARD TO BRING THE HOTEL INTO A MORE MODERN ERA, WITH UPDATED ROOMS AND BETTER FOOD.

Alfred and Marjorie Hall had learned a lot in the years about how to attract tourists.

In this brochure, they show off the modern rooms, point out the lovely setting, and brag about the swimming, the boating, and the fishing. Today's guests still value each of these things, including what the Halls described as "enchantment at every turn."

COME TO THE

HARBOR VIEW HOTEL

Come to the HARBOR VIEW HOTEL where the appetite gains a new edge and sleep a new peace. Located on Starbuck's Neck, at the entrance to Edgartown Harbor, the hotel is just a few blocks from the center of the shopping district of one of New England's oldest towns. A short stroll past historic whaling houses takes you to the shops, where you will find offerings for the luxury-minded, the collector, or for casual items of everyday living.

Speaking of dining . . . Your meals are meals of plenty, not only in quantity of servings, but also in pleasing variety. Fresh fish and shellfish, New England chowder for those who like the traditional Island dishes. Choice cuts, roasts, fresh vegetables and eggs from Island farms, good bread, rolls, muffins, pastries, baked in our own kitchens. Ample fare for each day's activities.

The HARBOR VIEW HOTEL takes pride in its spacious lawns and gardens. The hotel and cottages are provided with wide porches for outdoor enjoyment and ample lounging facilities, with fireplaces for your comfort and cheer indoors. The HARBOR VIEW HOTEL bears a name which means what it says — the view is of the harbor and seascape generally — and the property extends to the beach. Looking southerly you see the inner harbor and beyond that Katama Bay and South Beach. Easterly across the three-mile expanse of Old Great Harbor is Cape Pogue Light. Shift your glance a bit northerly and there is the open sea. Nothing obstructs your view as your eye ranges from inner harbor to the ocean sweep beyond Cape Pogue.

In addition to the Main hotel and Annex there are six large cottages providing suites from two to six rooms with baths; making ideal accommodations for families.

Service is our watchword. For your convenience there are telephones in every room. For your safety the hotel is completely equipped with an *Automatic Sprinkler System.* Room service is yours for the asking. Competent and willing employees are at your service at all hours, day or night.

COME TO MARTHAS VINEYARD

TO FIND YOUR OWN ISLAND PARADISE:
Swimming in surf or tranquil water warmed by sun and sand. Bathe directly from the hotel or the Beach Club.

For the fisherman. Your sport may vary from surf casting to deep sea sword or tuna fishing.

Golf and tennis are available at nearby clubs. The Island offers three excellent Golf Clubs.

Boats may be hired in any class. Sail it yourself or obtain the service of a proficient captain.

Transportation may be by air, by rail or car and boat. The Island offers enchantment at every turn. Bring your own car for trips afield, or rent one locally for your stay. Bicycles may be hired for the entire family. Air service is not only to and from the Island, but also available for sightseeing trips to nearby points of interest.

MARTHA'S VINEYARD is steeped in tradition. Edgartown, the County seat, boasts gracious old whaling homes with their four-square beauty, ancestral widow's walks, informal gardens, ornate doorways and rose covered fences. A leisurely walk from the hotel takes you past these homes down the shady lanes to other interests in the town. A turn to the right brings you to the historical society which takes you back into the days of Moby Dick; a turn to the left brings you to the activities of the harbor. Activities of the harborfront are at the front door of the HARBOR VIEW HOTEL — they are there for you to see from the porches and even from your bedroom window. Here through the season the single stickers fan out in racing formation, power cruisers, tall-sparred schooners, big yachts pass in and out on summer parade. The fishing craft, as all through the year, put out to sea and return to their home port.

Within walking distance of the HARBOR VIEW HOTEL you will find churches of various sects for your Sunday worship, or weekday meditation.

COME TO EDGARTOWN
where the air is clean, the water is crystal clear, the beaches have no hot dog stands, and there isn't a billboard to be found.

For rates and further information write:
HARBOR VIEW HOTEL
At Starbuck's Neck • *Edgartown, Mass.*
Telephone Edg. 444

HARBOR VIEW HOTEL

SUN

SURF

SERVICE

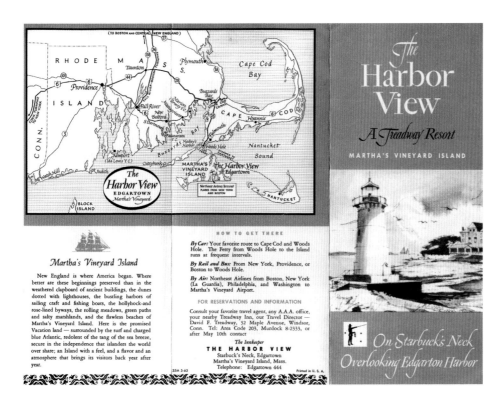

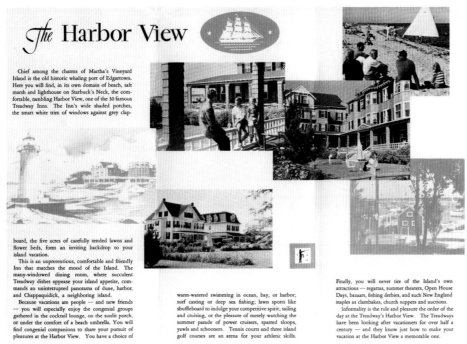

HARBOR VIEW BROCHURE
From 1950

For the first time in 1957 the Harbor View Hotel appeared in brochures of Treadway Inns together with other resort destinations in New England, New York, and Florida:

"EACH INN HAS ITS OWN PERSONALITY, ITS OWN SPECIAL ATTRACTIONS OFTEN REFLECTING AN IMPORTANT PERIOD OF YANKEE HISTORY, AND ALWAYS STRIVING FOR THE HIGHEST STANDARDS OF FOOD, WINE, AND SERVICE."

THE DANCING HALLS

Alfred Hall loved to dance. He and his
wife, Marjorie, continued to enjoy
dancing together well into their
retirement years at the Delray Beach
Club in Florida. That love of dancing,
his children say, most likely dated to
Hall's childhood memories of summer
evenings at the Harbor View Hotel.

Back in the years when his father was
growing up, says son, Buzz Hall, the
Harbor View held dances after dinner on
Sunday nights. The children would watch
and, as children do, they'd contrive to stay
up as late as possible. Buzz says his father
remembered the bedtime rule on those
nights of dancing:

"THE CHILDREN WERE
ALLOWED TO STAY FOR
THE MUSIC UNTIL THEY
COULD SEE THE FALL
RIVER LINE STEAMBOAT
COME AROUND
THE LIGHTHOUSE."

"OUR GOAL HAS BEEN ACCOMPLISHED"

Alfred Hall's life was an expression of seemingly boundless energy, but eventually even human dynamos wind down. He purchased the Harbor View with the intention of making it a fifteen-year project, and that's pretty much how it had worked out.

Hall, who had turned sixty-five in 1963, alerted his fellow owners of the Harbor View in a letter dated August 1965. "Our corporation was organized fifteen years ago," he wrote, "to restore the Harbor View Hotel to its former attractiveness and importance to Edgartown. . . . It is felt that our goal has been accomplished, and those of us who have been directing the affairs of the company would like to retire. This would seem to be an appropriate time to offer the property for sale."

Hall first asked his son if he might want to take over the hotel. Buzz Hall recalls, "I just said, 'Dad, the restaurant and hotel business is body and soul, and I don't know if I want to be tied down like that.'" Buzz Hall's great love has always been music, and as operator of the family's movie theatres for many years, he was known for bringing special off-season screenings of operas to the Island.

Alfred Hall turned next to a man twenty-six years his junior, an Edgartown native only a little older than his own children, an entrepreneur whose energy and devotion to his hometown echoed his own: Robert J. Carroll, known universally as Bob.

The hotel lobby as redecorated by Marjorie Hall, with floral drapes from F. Schumacher & Co., New York.

The Stars & Mr. Hall

Gregory Peck was a visitor to the Vineyard during the years the Halls regularly premiered new movies.

As the years of the postwar economic boom extended, the Harbor View was assuming a new prominence on the national stage. A new breed of movie celebrities discovered Martha's Vineyard, and Alfred Hall's connection to them was twofold: not only did he operate the Island's grandest resort hotel, he also owned and operated all the Island's movie houses.

Katharine Hepburn, who was often at the hotel, shown in one of her famous roles.

One of the first stars to become a seasonal Islander was James Cagney, whose Vineyard home had formerly belonged to Colonel Claghorn, a builder of the USS *Constitution* and an ancestor of Hall's wife, Marjorie. Cagney became an insurance client of Hall, and a visitor to the Hall theaters, where such classics as *Dinner at Eight, Grand Hotel,* and *Gone with the Wind* were screened to reserved-seat audiences.

Gregory Peck visited, and in 1942 Hall persuaded the author Somerset Maugham, then a seasonal Vineyarder, to host a wartime world premiere of the film based on his novel, *The Moon and Sixpence,* at Hall's movie theatre on Main Street in Edgartown. The *Vineyard Gazette* promised, "The event will bring together a neighborly gathering of the Island's own celebrities along with the off-Island press. The Island's first World Premiere will not follow tradition in all respects. There will be no bright lights, partly because of the [wartime] dim-out but partly because the theatre does not boast an electric sign."

Variety Magazine had great fun covering the Vineyard premiere, noting that by Hall's decree, such celebrities as Elizabeth Taylor and Ruth Gordon, Jimmy Cagney, American statesman Dean Acheson, and *New York Times* film critic Bosley Crowther had to wait in line for their movie tickets just like everyone else.

"Suppose I let a Crowther in," Hall said to the reporter from *Variety*. "What will I do with the other celebrities? So my rule is hard and fast. The only exception I make is for my wife. And even then some customers complain.

"So I say to them, 'Would you tell your wife to get to the end of the line?'"

The current Hall family still owns three theatres on the Vineyard, although none are functioning.

Katharine Hepburn, one of the most famous actors of modern times, was a regular guest of the Harbor View—sometimes bringing along her niece, Catherine Houghton, who played the ingénue opposite Sidney Poitier in *Guess Who's Coming to Dinner.*

Hepburn retreated to the Harbor View after the death of Spencer Tracy, and at the Harbor View she first read—and became enthralled by—the script for what would be one of her most famous films, *The Lion in Winter.* Its story of King Henry II's attraction to two women, his wife and mistress, resonated strongly with the actress who knew what it meant to be caught in a triangle with a married man.

Buzz Hall recalls that Kate Hepburn used to call his father "the Saint," and that he was mystified by the nickname until famous director Garson Kanin explained it to him: "Garson told me, 'Katharine had eyes for your father. She made a pass at him once, and he refused her in such a nice way—"you're a very lovely woman," he said, "but I'm in love with Marjorie." After that, he was the Saint.'"

1965
– TO –
1986

Young Bob Carroll, at far right, carries the flag in Edgartown's Independence Day Parade.

BOB CARROLL: A BLUEBIRD IN CONTROL

1965–1986

A self-made man of seemingly boundless energy stewards the hotel through two decades.

Bob Carroll was born in 1924 in the Jernegan house on South Summer Street, across from the *Vineyard Gazette* (and now part of the Charlotte Inn). His father, Rosario, worked as a butcher and struggled with a drinking problem all his life, dying at age fifty-nine; his mother, Mary, was a devout Catholic and a maid at the Charlotte Inn—which until 1934 had been a grocery before being converted to a summer inn.

Young Robert was, by his own description, one of the street urchins of Edgartown. But Alfred Hall, who would later be a friend and mentor, noticed him early as one of the brightest children in school and a member of the most advanced reading group. "Alfred and Henry Beetle Hough [the influential editor of the *Vineyard Gazette*], were on the

school committee together," Carroll says. "Henry told me a story from when I was in first or second grade: 'Alfred told me, "Look at that brat over there. He's a bluebird, and my niece is just a robin."'"

When he enlisted in the army after high school and registered the highest scores in his group on the military entrance exams, he was urged to enter Officer Training School—but refused, preferring to be in the thick of things. "I was probably stupid," he says now, "but I didn't want to lead groups. I was nineteen years old, and I ended up in the invasion of Iwo Jima." He earned a Bronze Star.

Back in Edgartown, he married Lucille Gardner Hillman in the fall of 1950—their marriage would last a quarter-century and yield four daughters—but to say that Bob Carroll, a man of seemingly constant restless energy, had settled down would be a stretch.

Dino Giamatti, who managed the Harbor View for Carroll for three summers from 1968 to 1970 and went on to spend his whole career in the hotel business, remembers him as a mentor and a bigger-than-life figure.

"THESE GUYS ON THE VINEYARD, THEY WORKED HARD, THEY PLAYED HARD, THEY PARTIED HARD. HE WAS QUITE A GUY WHEN I KNEW HIM—HE LIKED THE GIRLS, NO QUESTION ABOUT IT. HE WAS A CHARACTER. AN EXTRAORDINARILY ENTREPRENEURIAL MAN—HE HAD THIS ABSOLUTE FEEL FOR DOING THINGS, AND NO SHAME IN JUMPING IN AND BUYING A HOTEL WHEN HE KNEW BASICALLY NOTHING ABOUT IT. HE'D FIND THE RIGHT PEOPLE AND GO BY THE SEAT OF HIS PANTS. HE TRUSTED US YOUNGER FELLOWS—I WAS ONLY TWENTY-FIVE WHEN HE MADE ME MANAGER, AND HIS CHEFS AT THE SEAFOOD SHANTY WERE ALL YOUNG MEN. HE HAD GREAT FAITH IN YOUTH AND WAS VERY SUPPORTIVE."

Dino Giamatti

In a 2012 interview, Carroll, then eighty-nine, told *Martha's Vineyard Magazine,* "I don't work in moderation, I don't play in moderation, and I don't even chase women in moderation."

In his earlier years, Carroll admits, he didn't drink in moderation either. Now he divides his life story into two chapters: his drinking years and the years after he stopped. One of his proudest accomplishments was celebrating sixty years of sobriety in January 2013. Looking back, he says that the clarity and energy he found after giving up alcohol at age twenty-nine came almost as a revelation to him: "I discovered that after I stopped drinking, I could do almost anything."

STARTING WITH BORROWED MONEY

In 1965, when Alfred Hall approached him about buying the Harbor View, Carroll had one notable business accomplishment to his credit—the creation, four years earlier, and subsequent success of the Seafood Shanty restaurant on the Edgartown harbor front.

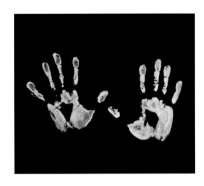

CHEF WEBER AND THE WHITE HANDPRINT

Chef Willie Weber, who followed Chef Henry Haller at the Harbor View, ran the hotel kitchen with an iron fist (as his wife, Marie, ran the dining room) during the days when the hotel operated on the American plan—with full meal service packaged into the rooms' fee. The Webers were part of the Treadway Inns management chain; every fall, winter, and spring, they worked at Mount Holyoke College, where he ran the student dining service.

"Willie Weber was a tough boss," says Norm Vunk, who managed the hotel for many of those years. "But I had an advantage with him because I had studied at the Culinary Institute, and he knew I could cook and run a kitchen. Willie was from Switzerland and trained in the great hotels of Switzerland and France. In stature he was short and robust, with a little mustache, and he watched everything like a hawk."

The handprint was a Willie Weber trademark, Norm remembers: "He would dip his hand in flour, and as a waitress was going into the dining room with her black skirt, he'd give her a little pat—and of course a handprint would go on her skirt. You couldn't do anything like that nowadays, but the girls used to think of it as kind of a badge of honor to have Willie's handprint."

"We all know that the Vineyard is unique, and we want to keep her that way, a difficult task to perform as the Island is 'discovered' by more and more people. I believe that the Vineyard is bound to grow, but the danger is that she will grow in an undisciplined and eventually ruinous manner."

BOB CARROLL

Bob Carroll (left) and friend Kenny Grant at about fourteen. (Bob's daughter Sue and Kenny's son Jerry are now married.)

"Alfred Hall liked me," says Carroll. "He was my friend. He called me one day and he said, 'You ought to buy the Harbor View Hotel.' I said, 'I'd love to, but I don't have any money.' He said, 'Maybe you can work that out.'"

Carroll didn't have much cash in 1965, but he did have good credit and a solid standing in civic life—as an Edgartown selectman, a county commissioner, and a member of several banks and community service organizations. Looking back on his career in business, he cites one simple practice as a secret of his success that endeared him especially to bankers: "I always paid my bills on time."

When he decided to buy the Harbor View, he went to the Plymouth Savings Bank, where he'd done business before, asking for a $250,000 loan. The actual price was $225,000, but Carroll knew he'd need extra money to staff and provision the hotel.

The Harbor View Hotel Co. Inc. came into being, and—in a decision Carroll would later regret—he brought in as his partner State Senator Allan F. Jones of Hyannis, an owner of restaurants on Cape Cod and a frequent visitor to the Vineyard. The new owners purchased the hotel in November 1965.

The Harbor View, on the eve of its seventy-fifth anniversary, had its third set of owners, still depending heavily on local control.

NEW PLUMBING AND A MOTEL

It was a time when the pace of change was beginning to unsettle even the most ardent advocates of growth on Martha's Vineyard. Carroll acknowledged as much in his campaign statements during an unsuccessful run for the state legislature in 1964. "We all know that the Vineyard is unique," he wrote, "and we want to keep her that way, a difficult task to perform as the Island is 'discovered' by more and more people. I believe that the Vineyard is bound to grow, but the danger is that she will grow in an undisciplined and eventually ruinous manner."

Announcing the sale of the Harbor View Hotel in 1965, the *Vineyard Gazette* reassured its readers that the new owners planned no major changes. "There will be some refurbishing of the existing facilities, Carroll said, but it is the intention of the owners to maintain the nostalgic charm of family hotels of an earlier day."

One of the first things he changed was the layout of the hotel rooms. When flush toilets had been installed during the 1920s—replacing the chamber pots that Carroll inherited by the dozens when he bought the hotel—they'd placed bathrooms at the front of the building, blocking the prized views of the lighthouse and harbor. "The best way to get the view from here was to sit on the throne and look out the window," he says. "Can you believe that?"

Another early initiative, in 1967, was as a pair of decidedly family-friendly construction projects, the first major additions to the Harbor View Hotel in more than half a century. In the place of the hotel's shuffleboard courts, Carroll had a swimming pool installed—and beside it, a three-story, 51-unit motel building.

The new motel building was patterned less after the original Harbor View buildings than after the motor inns that by now lined highways all across America—a boxlike structure beside the new pool, it packed seventeen twin-bedded rooms, each seventeen feet by fifteen feet and

with its own electric wall heater, into each floor. These motel units were a hit with the public right away, Carroll says, paying for themselves in the first two years.

Now with 143 rooms, the Harbor View's new owners had 51 more opportunities to generate income on each day of a short resort season. And Carroll pushed hard to extend the traditional three-month season by bringing groups for conferences in the spring and fall.

"I'M SURE THERE WERE TIMES WHEN BOB TOOK CARE OF LITTLE THINGS AND I NEVER KNEW ABOUT IT, BUT THERE WERE SOME PRETTY HEAVY-DUTY POLITICIANS WHO WOULD COME DOWN TO THE ISLAND AND STAY HERE; BOB WOULD ASK ME TO PICK THEM UP AT THE AIRPORT, AND THE WOMEN THEY WERE WITH WEREN'T NECESSARILY THEIR WIVES."

Norm Vunk, Bob Carroll's hotel manager

"WE KNEW WE HAD TO
EXTEND THE SEASON, WE
HAD TOO MUCH INVESTED,
AND THE WEATHER WAS
SO GOOD."

Bob Carroll

PUSHING THE SEASON

Getting the Harbor View prepared for a new season after nine months dormancy was always a scramble, Carroll recalls. "I remember the first convention we had was an MIT reunion in June. The head of the alumni group got here on a Wednesday or a Thursday, and he said, 'You son of a bitch, everyone's getting here Friday and this place looks like a dump.' I said, 'Wait 'til Friday.' I had all these college kids around, and he came over Friday afternoon and said, 'I don't know how the hell you did it, but you got this place together.'"

As it turned out, the Island had certain advantages as a setting for conventions and association meetings. "It's a sort of closed environment," Carroll explains with a grin. "When you get here, you can't get in any trouble that we can't get you out of in half an hour." And because his post as an Edgartown selectman from 1960 to 1970 also made him a police commissioner, Carroll was uniquely positioned to help any getting-out-of-trouble along when the occasion arose.

Carroll expanded his holdings by purchasing the Kelley House in 1973, with its fifty-six rooms a block from Main Street in Edgartown. And for his own use, he had the

Harbor View's attic space expanded into a three-thousand-square-foot penthouse apartment with breathtaking views of the town, the harbor, and the lighthouse.

Carroll, who would own the Harbor View Hotel for twenty-one years, doesn't regret a day of the experience. "A hotel is a fun thing," he says. "Here at the Harbor View, you meet people that you'd never meet in your life.

"I used to hang around at the front desk when I owned it, and some of the things people would ask you were crazy. One day we had a guy borrow an iron from us so he could iron his pants. Then he burned a hole in his pants, and he wanted to know what we were going to do about it."

Carroll is proud of his record as a self-made man, from modest beginnings to an honored civic and business leader in Edgartown. He still likes to recall the time when the chasm between the townies and the summer folk seemed impossibly vast, and he was on the wrong side of it: "When I was a kid, I remember seeing the natives tipping their hats to the summer people."

And so he cherishes the story of the elderly lady, the mother of a federal judge, who summered each year at the

Bob Carroll as a young boy with his mother, Mary, who worked as a maid at the Charlotte Inn.

"A hotel is a fun thing," says Carroll.

Harbor View: "She played golf every day, sat down and got drunk every night, and climbed up the stairs on her hands and knees. I remember when I bought the hotel, she asked me, 'Do you know Mary Carroll?' I said, 'Yeah, she's my mother.' She said, 'Oh.' My mother had been her maid at the Charlotte Inn.

"Every two or three days, she'd ask me again. She just couldn't understand how Mary Carroll's son could own the Harbor View Hotel."

And he recalls how his father, the butcher, once was friends with the Harbor View chef, and how sometimes in September when the dining room closed, the Carroll family would get the season's leftovers—"all sorts of things we never had at home," he says—from the hotel kitchen.

What Bob Carroll does regret, looking back, is taking Senator Jones as a business partner and selling the hotel to the senator's son in 1986. "When I was buying the Harbor View," he says, "I thought I needed a partner. Have you ever made a decision that cost you all your life?" He shakes his head: "I never should have sold the Harbor View. I should have bought my partner out, kept it, and turned the whole thing into condos, except for the motel."

Carroll was sixty-two years old when he got out of the hotel business for good. Norman Vunk, then the managing director of both hotels and Carroll's associate for the past twenty years, said, "Mr. Carroll is going to slow down a little bit, and I am really happy for him. I think he has been a real asset to the town, and I think everything he has done has been an improvement to the town."

In his sale to Harborview Associates in 1986, Carroll negotiated one provision that would cement his association with Edgartown's grandest hotel: a lifetime tenancy in his penthouse atop the Harbor View.

WHEN CHANGE CAME
TO MARTHA'S VINEYARD

THE 1960s WERE A DECADE OF DRAMATIC CHANGE NOT ONLY FOR
THE HARBOR VIEW BUT ALSO FOR MARTHA'S VINEYARD.

*Sen. Edward Kennedy and his wife, Joan, on the steps of the Edgartown court-
house, at the inquest into the death of Mary Jo Kopechne.*

In a way, it was the end of a more innocent era. Dino Giamatti, who managed the Harbor View for three summers
from 1968 to 1970, recalls that on his watch, the hotel ended
its long-established practice of feeding news items to the
social columnist of the local paper.

"Before it became something you shouldn't do, we used to
feed news to the newspaper—names of guests who were in for
a week or two, any other tidbit that was interesting. But then,
of course, we had to stop it because there were liability prob-
lems." Criminals might read the papers to see who wasn't at
home, so they could burglarize their houses, Giamatti
explains—or it might turn out that the woman So-and-So
was vacationing with at the Harbor View wasn't his wife.

The motel units added to the Harbor View over the winter of 1967—and the throng of national press that descended,
filling the new motel, after Senator Kennedy's accident on
Chappaquiddick in July 1969—changed the rhythms of life
at the hotel, Giamatti says: "The motel did change the personality of the hotel, which I thought was unfortunate—
because I was so accustomed to the old hotel and its gracious
way of doing things."

Looking back on the tumultuous 1960s from the vantage
point of January 1970, the *Vineyard Gazette* wrote, "And at
the end of the decade, two major pieces of unfinished business—the inquest into the death of Mary Jo Kopechne
when a car driven by Sen. Edward M. Kennedy plunged into
Pocha Pond, and the trials of dozens of teenagers arrested
for possession and selling of drugs."

And Along Comes

A BIG SHARK

"I'll catch this bird for you, but it ain't gonna be easy. Bad fish. Not like going down the pond chasin' bluegills and tommycods. This shark, swallow you whole. . . . And we gotta do it quick, that'll bring back your tourists, put all your businesses on a payin' basis. But it's not gonna be pleasant."

CAPTAIN QUINT (ROBERT SHAW)

Jaws 1 *and* 2 *were both made on the Vineyard, and turned Edgartown and other sections of the Island into ready-made sets for the big shark with the mean streak.*

As much as Bob Carroll enjoyed owning the Harbor View, he says it was never a big moneymaker. "I'm not sure the Harbor View Hotel has ever made real money. You keep thinking it's going to turn around and make money, but I had to borrow each year to make renovations."

In 1974, with the expenses of buying and expanding the Kelley House weighing heavy on his books, Carroll was closer than ever to violating his personal code of paying every bill on time. But then came financial salvation in the sort of windfall we expect only from Hollywood. A young filmmaker named Steven Spielberg was planning to make a movie on Martha's Vineyard. Its name was *Jaws*.

When the director's advance team contacted Carroll, he had already learned the lesson that no commodity is more perishable than a hotel room for a given night. He'd been burned, and badly, when the national press corps had made reservations for Senator Edward Kennedy's date in court after the Chappaquiddick accident in which Mary Jo Kopechne had died. That court date was postponed, and the hotel didn't see a penny.

He says, "One of the things I discovered, early on, was that if you got a bad weather forecast, everyone who had reservations would call and cancel. I started asking for security deposits, nonrefundable."

When the *Jaws* team called to reserve fifty rooms, Carroll demanded a $25,000 deposit and got it. He estimates that by the time filming was done, he and his various Edgartown enterprises—which by then included the two hotels; the Seafood Shanty restaurant; Edgartown Marine, which helped outfit the boats shooting scenes on the water; and his Carroll & Vincent Realty business, which arranged pricey rentals for key members of the movie crew—made more than $1 million from the filming of *Jaws*. "That," he says, "was a wonderful experience."

Not exactly wonderful, but certainly memorable, was the food fight that broke out at the Harbor View in that summer of 1974 as director Spielberg and his cast blew off steam from a memorably difficult production season. How exactly it started—who threw the first meatball or handful of mashed potatoes—no one can exactly recall. But bartender George Gamble later said the principals were Spielberg and actors Roy Scheider and Richard Dreyfuss. "The three managed to make a real mess," he said. "It was a disgusting sight, seeing them covered in ravioli, cake, and diced fruit." According to one account of the fracas, the combatants rinsed off by jumping into the Harbor View pool.

Nearly four decades after the success of *Jaws*, the money continues to trickle in. Carroll, who was cast as a selectman in the fictional town of Amity, gets regular residual checks from the blockbuster film, which to date has earned a total of nearly $2 billion.

Top: Bob Carroll, who actually did serve Edgartown as a selectman, played a selectman in the fictional town of Amity for the film Jaws. *Bottom: A* Jaws *film crew member edits in one of the Harbor View rooms.*

WHEN THE *JAWS* TEAM CALLED TO RESERVE FIFTY ROOMS, CARROLL DEMANDED A $25,000 DEPOSIT AND GOT IT.

1986
– TO –
1989

SCANDAL AND RENAISSANCE

1986–1989

*Under the new owners, things began to go bad
at the Harbor View almost from the beginning.
Bankruptcy was just two years away.*

The new owners of the Harbor View were something of a high-flying bunch.

Senator Allan Jones, who had been Bob Carroll's partner in the original purchase of the hotel, was a veteran state legislator who represented the Cape and Islands for two decades, winning his first election to state office in 1948 at the age of twenty-six. Like Carroll, he was a veteran of World War II; unlike Carroll, Senator Jones was a Republican who served fourteen terms as a state representative and then another eight as a state senator.

The new ownership group included his son, Stephen C. Jones, and Robert Welch. These three men, from offices in Hyannis, owned six hotels on the Vineyard, on Cape Cod,

and in Maine, and they also operated a small regional airline named Gull Air.

For the first time in its history, the Harbor View was now owned entirely by off-Island interests. But Norm Vunk, who had managed the hotel for a decade under Bob Carroll, was a company man who had "put heart and soul" into the Harbor View. He'd come to work there at age twenty-five, when Carroll had plucked him from the kitchen of the Seafood Shanty, which Carroll also owned. He'd loved the hotel for the fourteen years he worked there.

The Harbor View was a little fusty then, with its painted floors and the dark wallpaper on its horsehair plaster walls. "It wasn't anything modern," he says, "but the people who

"THERE'S THIS INSTANT GRATIFICATION WHEN THINGS ARE GOING RIGHT AND PEOPLE ARE HAPPY; THERE'S NOTHING LIKE IT. AND I'LL TELL YOU, WHEN THINGS AREN'T RIGHT, THERE ISN'T ANYTHING WORSE. BUT AT THE HARBOR VIEW, PEOPLE WERE HAPPY MOST OF THE TIME. YOU COME UP NORTH WATER STREET AND BANG, HERE'S THIS HOTEL, THERE'S THE LIGHTHOUSE AND CHAPPAQUIDDICK AND THE WATER. EVERYONE KIND OF MELLOWS A LITTLE BIT."

Norm Vunk

came back year after year were used to it. We were dealing with old blue-blood money in those days. The little old ladies, as we used to call them, were there from mid-June until Labor Day. They used to fight over who got the windows with the best view. I remember a Mrs. Comstock had the prime one for years and, boy, nobody could take that away."

Vunk worked twelve-hour days and seven-day weeks all summer, then supervised renovations to the Harbor View during the winter seasons, including renovations to the main hotel's bathrooms, the installation of central air-conditioning, creation of a basement laundry operation, and the conversion of the hotel attic into Carroll's new and distinctive penthouse apartment.

So when the new, "foreign" owners took over the hotel in 1986, Vunk stayed on. Even though the owners were new, their names were familiar to him and other Islanders. He figured it would be business as usual.

A Bad Moment of Worry and Tears

Things began to go bad almost from the beginning. Vunk lasted only weeks in the new owners' employ. "They wanted me to do things with money, with the books, and they told me, 'Whatever happens, we'll take the fall.' I was really shook up. I went to Bob Carroll with tears in my eyes and I said, 'I can't do this.' He said, 'Don't worry about it, don't look back—get out.' Which I did."

Over the next two years, from his penthouse apartment, Carroll watched as the enterprise he'd nurtured for more than two decades hurtled toward bankruptcy.

The new partners almost immediately began to rack up debt at an alarming rate. Gull Air went bankrupt in March 1987. The Edgartown National Bank placed a lien of $300,000 on the Harbor View for money owed to it by the new partnership. The advertising agency for the Regency Inns chain, which had been hired to manage the Harbor View, was owed $550,000 in unpaid advertising bills. The IRS filed a federal tax lien for nearly $50,000 in unpaid taxes. Carroll also filed suit, demanding the $1.6 million the new owners owed to him for a second mortgage he held on the Harbor View and Kelley House hotels.

In March 1988 the National Home Life Assurance Co. filed suit against Harborview Associates for default on the $11.5 million mortgage that covered the two hotel properties. That June 2, the court authorized the Missouri-based finance company to foreclose. On August 2, just hours before a scheduled public

Reports in June 1988 showed

ALLAN JONES
in default for

$3.4 M

STEPHEN JONES
owing seven separate creditors

$2.6 M

ROBERT WELCH
in default on debts of

$2.6 M

THIS DID NOT INCLUDE THE NEW HOTEL DEBT THEY'D TAKEN ON IN 1986.

VOICES

THE TIME OF OUR LIVES

"My memories of the Harbor View go back to my high school days, when Bob Carroll's daughter, Sue, was one of my classmates. They would have these huge weddings at the hotel—I remember one two-day wedding where we were all working in the kitchen, and we had the time of our lives. There was leftover food—we got to drink wine from the bottles that hadn't been emptied—it was just the best time going. At the end, I remember the tip we got for the work was twice as much as we earned for washing dishes and cleaning up."

GREG ORCUTT
Manager of Vineyard radio station WMVY

auction of the two hotels, Harborview Associates filed for bankruptcy protection, averting the sale.

What had gone so dramatically, precipitously wrong? An examiner's report prepared for the federal bankruptcy court summed up the situation bluntly: "Essentially, the cash generated from the Harbor View and Kelley House have been used for the benefit of related entities."

Or, as Bob Carroll describes it, "They had all the money sent over to them in Hyannis. When they went under, they owed me four and a half, five million dollars."

Stephen Jones and Robert Welch were eventually convicted and went to jail on charges of bank fraud, forgery, and conspiracy for their efforts to keep their enterprises afloat during the years leading to the Harbor View's bankruptcy.

Stephen Richmond, the Boston attorney appointed by the court as bankruptcy trustee for the Harbor View and Kelley House, hired a new general manager and worked through the summer and fall of 1988 to put proper financial controls in place.

Both hotels remained open as dates for their sale at auction were pushed back repeatedly—Richmond explaining that he wanted first to stabilize operations as much as possible. In December 1988 he announced an agreement to sell the two hotels to National Home, holder of the first mortgage, for $13,247,740. But the court disallowed that sale, hoping to be able to recover more at public auction.

Finally, in April 1989 the Harbor View and Kelley House hotels got their day on the block at a public auction held in one of the Harbor View's first-floor meeting rooms. It took three tries before Arthur J. Halleran Jr., chairman of First Winthrop Corp., a real estate syndication firm, placed a winning bid for both the Kelley House and the Harbor View. The $12.3 million sale price—about sixty cents on the dollar when set against the properties' assessed value—meant there wouldn't be money to pay off anything but the debt to National Home, holder of the first mortgage. Holders of second mortgages, including Carroll and the Edgartown National Bank, got nothing.

The darkest period in the history of the Harbor View was over. As disappointed as he must have been at the sale price, Carroll said at the end of the auction:

"I'M VERY PLEASED WITH THE NEW OWNERS. I DON'T THINK THEY COULD HAVE HAD A BETTER BUYER."

BIG MONEY ARRIVES

In First Winthrop, the Harbor View Hotel had an owner unlike any it had ever had.

Created in 1975 and led since 1977 by the Harvard-educated financier Arthur J. Halleran Jr., Winthrop owed its existence to the fine print of the U.S. tax code. Winthrop was one of a large field of enterprises, known as real estate syndicators, that flourished from the 1970s into the mid-1980s. For First Winthrop and Halleran, whose owlishly large glasses gave him the look of a financial boy wonder, the Harbor View was their first venture into Vineyard real estate; the firm was already heavily invested in commercial properties on Nantucket.

Winthrop's business was investing other people's money in real estate. For each new deal, Winthrop would create a syndicate and sell shares to wealthy investors, managing properties on their behalf. The beauty of the tax law in those days was that when investors saw profits, they were profits—and when they saw losses, every penny could be subtracted directly from other income.

Properly set up—and no company was better at the game of purchase and leaseback than First Winthrop—an investment in one of Halleran's real estate syndicates simply had no downside. In 1984, the company's peak year before the tax laws changed, Winthrop's real estate partnerships brought in $725 million of investors' money.

Under Halleran's leadership, Winthrop had profits consistently doubling each year during its first decade. But then came a double whammy: Washington rewrote the tax code in 1986, ending the favored status of real estate investments. Suddenly, investments that had been held more for their tax-advantaged status than for their inherent profitability were a lot less valuable to people with high incomes. And soon after came the great commercial real estate recession of the early 1990s, which cut heavily into the value of real estate portfolios and arrested the steady climb in rents that could be charged.

WINTHROP'S CLEAR INTENT FROM THE DAY OF THE PURCHASE WAS TO TAKE THE HARBOR VIEW UP-MARKET, POSITIONING IT FOR THE FIRST TIME AS AN EXCLUSIVE DESTINATION IN A SOUGHT-AFTER ISLAND SETTING. AND WHAT WINTHROP BROUGHT TO THIS PROJECT WAS EXACTLY WHAT THE HARBOR VIEW NEEDED AS IT APPROACHED THE CENTURY MARK—A WILLINGNESS TO SPEND MONEY ON WHATEVER SCALE WAS NECESSARY TO RESTORE AND IMPROVE ITS COMMERCIAL PROPERTIES.

First Winthrop was one of the only large real estate syndicators to survive the shakeout of 1986, because Halleran had seen it coming. In 1985 he bought control of Winthrop from his forty partners, scaled back sharply, and reinvented the company with a focus on buying and managing unique, high-end properties. After shifting away from tax-oriented deals before the law changed in 1986, Winthrop saw its income from property management jump from 1 percent to more than 60 percent of all revenue.

By the time of its purchase of the Harbor View and Kelley House in 1989, Winthrop held an asset mix worth an estimated $6.5 billion and had successfully syndicated more than 250 separate real estate ventures. In 1984 Winthrop had purchased nineteen buildings in New York, comprising 4.5 million square feet and including proper-

ties on Fifth and Park Avenues. In 1985, after spending more than $150 million on renovations, Winthrop syndicated its $430 million investment for $757 million to eleven hundred investors who contributed $250,000 each. Among those investors were producer George Lucas, movie stars Woody Allen and Lily Tomlin, and Pennsylvania senator John Heinz. At the time, it was the largest real estate private placement ever done in the United States.

Notable among its other assets was Winthrop's $55 million purchase in 1986 of some 160 commercial properties in downtown Nantucket from Walter Beinecke, an heir to the S&H Green Stamps fortune.

In the Harbor View, First Winthrop saw everything it was looking for in a property acquisition: a bargain with great potential, in a mature market relatively safe from new

SUSAN & PHIL MERCIER

Susan Mercier worked just one summer at the Harbor View Hotel in 1984, but it was a season well-spent. She learned to clean rooms, and she met her husband, Phil. They married two years after they met and live in Edgartown. He's a banker, and she manages Edgartown Books.

"I came to the Island to visit a friend, and her family let me live in their toolshed. Three or four days into my vacation I got a job at the Harbor View as a chambermaid. I wanted to make some extra money babysitting, so one night I went to a room where a tremendously tall guy and his lovely, tiny wife, were waiting with their daughter. Turns out it was [Celtics' basketball star] Kevin McHale.

"When I took their little girl out to the pool, all these sports guys were sitting around, waiting to go to some cocktail party and were friendly because they knew the little girl. Phil, who had worked at the housekeeping department of the Harbor View for years, was looking out the window at all these sports stars. I caught his eye, and he asked me out."

A leisurely moment on a summer's day in the waters in front of the hotel.   *The view from the Edgartown lighthouse.*

competitors. "Your greatest potential gain is in buying something nobody else wants," explained Clinton Glass, project manager for the hotel's restoration, in an interview for *Contract Design* magazine.

"Then you ask, 'Who do we want to come back, and what must we do to make them come back? And if we can take it to a certain level, what can we get for room rates?' That defines the limits of what you can do."

But in that first summer of 1989, the goal of its new owners was simply to keep the Harbor View and Kelley House open. "We know this year isn't going to be highly profitable," said David Ling, Winthrop's vice president for hotel operations, "but that's all right. We knew it would be wrong not to open the hotels."

All that summer, Winthrop had one eye on the daily life of the Harbor View Hotel and another on the massive off-season project that would begin after its closing on September 30: a $5.5 million renovation intended to modernize the hotel while restoring the hotel to its original Victorian grandeur.

"THE WELCOME ENTRY OF FIRST WINTHROP INTO THE VINEYARD TOURIST MARKET ENDED A LONG AND SAD CHAPTER OF DECLINE, MISMANAGEMENT, AND BANKRUPTCY FOR THESE TWO HOTELS SO CRITICAL TO A STABLE RESORT BUSINESS HERE. NOW, FINALLY, THE HARBOR VIEW HOTEL AND KELLEY HOUSE WILL HAVE THE FINANCIAL RESOURCES AND PROFESSIONAL BACKING NECESSARY TO RESTORE THE HISTORIC COMPLEX TO ITS ONCE COMMANDING POSITION AT THE CENTER OF THIS VINEYARD RESORT COMMUNITY."

Vineyard Gazette

SPORTS STARS

THE JOHN HAVLICEK CELEBRITY FISHING TOURNAMENT

BEGUN IN THE EARLY 1980S, HAS BEEN BASED AT THE HARBOR VIEW
FOR ALMOST EVERY ONE OF ITS MORE THAN THIRTY YEARS.

Baseball legend Joe DiMaggio in 1987 with John Havlicek, host of the charity fishing tournament based at the Harbor View.

AMONG ITS GUESTS
HAVE BEEN...

Phillies Third-Baseman
MIKE SCHMIDT

Astronaut
BRUCE MELNICK

Comedian
LENNY CLARKE

Basketball Hall of Famer
BOB COUSY

Colts Quarterback
JOHNNY UNITAS

NCAA Basketball Coach
BOBBY KNIGHT

Yankees Legend
JOE DIMAGGIO

The tournament has raised some $4 million for the Genesis Fund, a nonprofit organization committed to helping children with birth defects, genetic disorders, and intellectual disabilities and their families.

"These Rooms Are Particularly Desirable"

THE TRADITION OF COTTAGES AT THE HARBOR VIEW, WHICH NOW NUMBER SIX, GREW STRICTLY OUT OF JEALOUSY: OAK BLUFFS HAD THEM AND EDGARTOWN DIDN'T.

Cottages in connection with the Harbor View Hotel,
Edgartown, Mass.

Oak Bluffs, which until 1907 was called Cottage City, had built a huge resort economy based on the charming cottages erected on and around the Methodist camp-meeting grounds. Thousands of people came to the town throughout the summer, turning what was once sheep grazing land into a thriving resort.

Edgartown, feeling left out of the action, wanted its new hotel to offer the cottage way of life.

The first mention of cottages on the Harbor View campus appeared in a booklet printed for the 1896 season by hotel manager Frank Douglas. The booklet opened with lines of poetry by Longfellow extolling the joys of living

beside the sea and promised, "On every breath that blows from the surrounding waters, comes refreshing coolness, renewed life, healthful ozone."

Among the Harbor View's notable attractions in that summer of 1896 was this: "A cottage of twelve rooms, beautifully furnished, with all modern conveniences, is connected with the hotel for parties desiring the seclusion and quiet of cottage life. These rooms are particularly desirable. A competent person is constantly in charge."

Because the Harbor View campus encompassed nearly four acres, and because moving houses from place to place was so common as to be almost unremarkable on the Island

n those days, the hotel had accumulated six cottages by 920, when time came to inventory the property after the death of its owner, Dr. Thomas Walker. On Walker's schedule of real estate at the county courthouse, they are listed rather unromantically as Cottages No. 1 through 6, but with notes that suggest their provenance.

Cottages 1 (almost certainly the one mentioned in the 896 advertising), 4, and 6 were built where they stood for use by the Harbor View. Cottage 2, known in its early years as the Chadwick, was one of the grand captain's houses of North Water Street, originally built for Edward Wells Chadwick, purchased by Walker, and moved to the hotel campus sometime before 1910.

Cottage 3 was a wing of the old Mattakeset Lodge at Katama, built in 1873, closed in 1905, purchased and mostly torn down by Walker in 1910, its lumber salvaged for use at the hotel. The wing was moved over land a distance of several miles that winter.

Cottage 6, placed at the very back of the Harbor View property, was the Huxford, purchased by Walker in 1908 and moved from the lot that is now an open lawn between two of Edgartown's Main Street landmarks, the Old Whaling Church and the Dr. Daniel Fisher House.

Today, these simple Captain's Cottages have been reimagined as the ultimate in summer retreats—condominium suites of one-, two-, and three-bedroom design in five luxurious cottage buildings tucked into the freshly landscaped hotel grounds.

The new life for the cottages began in September 2012, when the Harbor View announced the release of a limited collection of eighteen fully serviced cottage suites that offered the rewards of Island ownership without the hassles.

The cottage program provides for full, deeded ownership that allows owners year-round access to their suites and the opportunity to participate in the hotel's year-round rental program, in essence adding the suites to the hotel room inventory when they are not in residence. The suites range in size from 435 to 1,473 square feet.

"The buyer drawn to the Captain's Cottages will be someone who appreciates the breadth of experiences available on the Vineyard and at Harbor View Hotel," says Masood Bhatti, managing member of the ownership group, Harborview Investors LLC. "For a fortunate few, these eighteen suites are an invitation to cross the threshold from indulging in the Vineyard lifestyle to owning it; from visiting the Island to belonging here and becoming part of its fabric."

1989
— TO —
2006

Sketch of the Harbor View by artist Dana Gaines, commissioned for the hotel's centennial.

A RETURN TO ITS "COMMANDING POSITION"

1989–2006

As the hotel's centennial nears, First Winthrop's restoration of the Harbor View aims at four-star excellence.

Things had changed on the Vineyard, particularly in Edgartown, and the First Winthrop renovation being planned was meant to reflect and capitalize on that. Or, as the *Vineyard Gazette* described it, the hotel needed to be returned to "its once commanding position at the center of this Vineyard resort community."

Over the summer of 1989, First Winthrop worked with experts from the Preservation Partnership, an architectural firm specializing in historic preservation, to research the Harbor View and prepare plans for its restoration. Winthrop brought in hotel planning consultants and an interior design team from the Westin Hotels group to assist with the project.

Much of the restoration begun that December involved work that, once completed, would be invisible—beginning below ground level, where more than ninety original brick-and-mortar support columns were replaced with reinforced concrete and steel. New heating, cooling, and electrical systems were installed; plumbing was replaced; and more than thirty tons of new structural steel replaced old wood framing inside the walls. Winthrop's renovation included adding the classic Victorian turrets on the Harbor View roofs, and a twelve-foot open porch was wrapped around the main building with a new gazebo placed prominently at the corner.

For the first time, the entire Harbor View was insulated and fitted with double-pane windows. "It is our

THE RENOVATION WON A FIRST-PLACE AWARD FROM THE AMERICAN SOCIETY OF INTERIOR DESIGNERS IN 1991 AND WAS NAMED THE OUTSTANDING CONSTRUCTION PROJECT OF THE YEAR IN 1992 BY THE ASSOCIATION OF GENERAL CONTRACTORS.

The Harbor View was listed in 1997 in Historic Hotels of America, a program of the National Trust for Historic Preservation for quality hotels that have faithfully maintained their historic integrity, architecture, and ambience. It's been on that elite short list ever since.

hope to extend the shoulder season so the Island's economy can become more stable," said Jonathan Louis, manager of the hotel.

By the end of June 1990 the last carpets were being laid and draperies hung, and employees were being trained for a soft opening in the first week of July. The hotel staff was expanded to 160 by mid-July—including many seasonal employees imported from colleges in Ireland, England, and Scotland.

A *Vineyard Gazette* reporter toured the new Harbor View with Louis in July, noting one now-quaint amenity that presaged the world-changing technologies to come: each guest room was newly fitted with separate telephone jacks for computer modems.

The level of excellence that First Winthrop's management team was looking for in its revitalization of the Harbor View was four-star hotel service, and they achieved it.

AFTER ONE HUNDRED YEARS IN BUSINESS, THE HARBOR VIEW SEEMED TO HAVE SEEN IT ALL, INCLUDING GOOD YEARS AND BAD, AND YET IT WAS STILL HANGING ON, READY TO CELEBRATE.

CENTENNIAL PREPARATIONS

First Winthrop was not yet through with its new historic properties, though.

As the Island's busy season of 1990 wound down, First Winthrop went back to work on its Edgartown properties, with a $1.5 million renovation of the Kelley House and a second, $2.2 million round of improvements at the Harbor View, this time focusing on the exterior grounds.

A brick walkway replaced what had been a road connecting North Water and Fuller Streets, dividing the Harbor View campus. The twenty-four-year-old swimming pool was torn out and replaced, and a storage bunker was hidden beneath an expanse of lawn and parking lot, accessed through the basement of a building at the very back of the property.

This was a time of economic distress for the United States—the inflation of the late 1980s and a sudden doubling in oil prices, triggered by the invasion of Kuwait, had created a mood of consumer pessimism. All across the Vineyard, owners of seasonal businesses worried that perhaps this year, the visitors might decide not to come.

But Carl Erickson, project manager for the Harbor View renovations, said during a tour of the property in April that bookings for 1991 were already up 40 percent. "We're all standing around," he said, saying, "What recession?"

Winthrop Loses Control

First Winthrop's purchase of the Harbor View and Kelley House in 1989 came at a moment that proved, in retrospect, to be a high-water mark for the investment company. Winthrop's ambitious renovations of the two hotels were among its last projects of that scope, as its financial fortunes began to turn.

The year 1990 saw Winthrop post a modest profit, but the firm incurred steady losses each year from 1991 through 1995.

Soon after acquiring the Harbor View, First Winthrop began looking for properties and parts of its business that it could spin off to raise cash. In 1994 Winthrop sold its resort and hotel management company to Interstate Hotels Corp., handing over the management to its Island hotels in mid-July.

By late 1994 Arthur Halleran, the chairman who had built First Winthrop into a real estate colossus over two decades, needed to sell control of First Winthrop to pay off its investors. He first attempted, but failed, to craft a deal with Apollo Real Estate Advisors, a part of New York financier Leon Black's corporate buyout enterprise which already owned 6 percent of Winthrop.

Late in 1994 Nomura Asset Capital Corp., a giant Japanese finance company, purchased a controlling interest in Winthrop from Halleran and his partners for $24.5 million—under an agreement that had Halleran heading the committee that would lead the company.

First Winthrop was a bite-sized acquisition for Nomura, then the largest security company in the world—four times larger than Merrill Lynch. In July 1995 Nomura sold its stake to Apollo, the firm that had been chasing after Winthrop the year before, and suddenly both Halleran and his vice chairman John Wexler were gone.

One token Winthrop executive was left on the management panel charting the future course of the firm's investments and divestments—Richard McCready, formerly Winthrop's general counsel and managing director. Speaking of Apollo, McCready admitted that July, "When all is said and done, they control the company. They're the owner."

Right: Making use of its place on the water, fishing and boating have long been part of the attraction and tradition of the Harbor View. As a 1950s marketing brochure promised, "To be surrounded by sand, surf, and sea is a delight you find outside our doors."

President Bill Clinton thanks Patricia Wheeler (right), for many years the concierge of the Harbor View, after his family's brunch.

A PRESIDENTIAL BRUNCH

Sunday brunch at the Harbor View has been a special occasion for Vineyarders and visitors for generations, and celebrities have not been strangers there. On August 29, 1993, with just half an hour's notice, the Harbor View served its most memorable guests ever when President Bill Clinton; wife, Hillary; and daughter, Chelsea, stopped by to enjoy a meal together. The occasion was the First Family's final meal on Martha's Vineyard after ten days of vacationing at a secluded estate in Edgartown. Their waiter was Vincent Walton of the dining room staff, a summer employee from Fort Lauderdale, Florida.

THE PRESIDENT STARTED WITH TWO GLASSES OF PEAR JUICE; CHELSEA ORDERED ORANGE JUICE, AND MRS. CLINTON EXPRESSED HERSELF DELIGHTED WITH HER GLASS OF FRESH WATERMELON JUICE, ISLAND-GROWN. SAUSAGE, BACON, AND EGGS WERE ENJOYED BY ALL, AND THERE WERE SECOND HELPINGS OF THE BREAD PUDDING PREPARED BY THE HARBOR VIEW'S PASTRY CHEF, LIZ KANE.

After brunch, the president spent several minutes with the staff, and the First Family summoned executive chef Deborah Huntley from the kitchen to thank her personally for the good food.

As the family was leaving, Jim Moore, director of restaurants for Winthrop Hotels & Resorts, and Geraldine Roddy, dining room supervisor, presented the president with a white Harbor View Clipper jacket. "We are confident that the jacket will be worn with pride during future golf excursions," the Harbor View wrote in a memorandum to its staff. "We look forward to the First Family's return to our special Island."

APOLLO CASHES IN

Not long after Apollo took over First Winthrop, the real estate sales began, and the Harbor View was little more than a burden for Apollo.

In June 1998 Winthrop's resort properties on Nantucket were sold to Jill and Stephen Karp of Weston, Massachusetts, for $33 million in one of the largest real estate transactions in that island's history. A few years later, the commercial and retail properties that made up the remainder of Winthrop's Nantucket portfolio were sold to the Karps as well.

A classic resort hotel like the Harbor View just didn't fit with the corporate DNA of Apollo Real Estate Advisors, the branch of Apollo Global Management whose main focus since 1993 had always been on high-risk, high-return investments.

The Apollo group continued to fly the First Winthrop banner over the Harbor View Hotel until the very end of its ownership. In November 2006 Peter Braverman, the president of Winthrop Realty Trust, announced that a buyer for the Harbor View and Kelley House had been found.

The new owner was Scout Real Estate Capital of Nantucket LLC. Its principal, Alan Worden, declared both his appreciation for the Harbor View Hotel and his intentions for the property in his first conversation with the *Vineyard Gazette*.

"The Harbor View and Kelley House are spectacular properties," he said. "We view them as irreplaceable assets, incredibly well located. The goal is to preserve the best architecture there and enhance it."

THREE-DAY CENTENNIAL

MORE THAN A THOUSAND PEOPLE ATTENDED THE CENTENNIAL CELEBRATION
OVER THE OCTOBER 4, 1991, WEEKEND TO COMMEMORATE THE HARBOR VIEW.
IT WAS A CELEBRATION OF BOTH THE HOTEL AND THE ISLAND.

A page from the commemorative edition put out by the Martha's Vineyard Times.

The massive restoration came just in time for a celebration of history that rekindled the community's love affair with the grand hotel at Starbuck Neck. The Harbor View's centennial, held the weekend of October 4, was a three-day festival featuring five-course Victorian banquets every night, the menu based on that of the opening celebration in 1891.

Visitors from the mainland and from every Island town came to enjoy the weekend events, which included an antique auto show, demonstrations by national nine-wicket croquet champion Reid Fleming, and serenades from the Prime Alliance, New England's championship barbershop quartet. On the hotel lawns, Island musician Nancy Jephcote played fiddle tunes, and hot dogs, ice cream cones, and lemonade sold by the hundreds at a special centennial price: five cents. In the evenings, David Crohan played ragtime piano, and the Fenway Ensemble of the Boston Chamber Society performed for the dinner guests, including Edgartown's full board of selectmen: Fred B. Morgan Jr., Dana Anderson, and Tom Durawa.

The *Martha's Vineyard Times*—the weekly paper Bob Carroll helped to start in 1984 as the result of a brutal fight over the land in front of the hotel—published a special commemorative edition, *The Centennial Times*. Its cover story was a colorful account of the Harbor View's birth that played heavily on Edgartown's early envy of Oak Bluffs as a successful summer resort.

The *Vineyard Gazette*'s correspondent marveled at the changes a century had brought: "It is hard to imagine that the Harbor View Hotel was once the sole structure in this area. Today the Harbor View is bounded to the sides and to the back by a sea of summer homes, white picket fences and green privet hedges."

Almost Wasn't

The vista that gave the Harbor View Hotel its name had been altered dramatically by the hurricane of 1938, and by the replacement of the old Edgartown Lighthouse in 1939 with a cast-iron Coast Guard tower barged in from Ipswich. The stretch of water between the lighthouse and shore, previously spanned by a wooden walkway popularly known as the Bridge of Sighs, began to fill in with sand. By the time Carroll acquired the Harbor View, the opening of Eel Pond on the land between the hotel and the water had shifted from the harbor side to the Nantucket Sound side, west to east.

Carroll, whose penthouse atop the Harbor View now offers the world's best perspective on the lighthouse and its surroundings, was the co-owner of those acres of bluffs and marsh along North Water Street with his partner, Senator Allan Jones. In 1973, the two men proposed to build two houses on the land across from their hotel.

Their plan—to complete the row of homes that stretches clear into town on the strip of land between the street and harbor—was the centerpiece of the most storied and longest-running battle between developers and environmentalists ever staged on Martha's Vineyard.

Carroll maintains that what he and Jones wanted to do with their two 1.5-acre lots was no more than what every other owner of harbor front property had been allowed to

do in that neighborhood. His problem was that by 1973 this open stretch, the last undeveloped land on North Water Street, offered the only remaining unobstructed views of the lighthouse—and though he owned that vista, it had become one of Edgartown's public treasures.

Henry Beetle Hough, editor of the *Vineyard Gazette,* led a ten-year campaign against Carroll's project that played out in jurisdictions ranging from Edgartown's local boards to the federal courts, taking so many twists and turns that they could easily fill a book. In fact, much of Hough's 1976 book, *To the Harbor Light,* covers the controversy.

Opponents of Carroll's building plans said they would destroy the coastal ecosystem and obstruct views of a landmark important to the tourist industry. Carroll dismissed the opponents as elitists who had their nice houses and didn't want him to have his.

Although Carroll won approvals from every local and state agency, including the Army Corps of Engineers, a determined group of fourteen Edgartown citizens battled on in the courts to stop the construction.

When opponents of the building project turned to the

wetlands near the harbor, they emphatically demurred. "I we stand up against this filling," then-selectman Edith Potter said, "Bob Carroll's going to sue us. If we do nothing, the other side will sue us."

Fairleigh S. Dickinson Jr., a philanthropist and Edgartown summer resident, finally stepped in to settle the fight In January 1984 Dickinson agreed to buy the Starbuck Neck property between the Harbor View and the lighthouse in a complicated transaction involving $525,000 and the transfer to Carroll of five historic properties on the Edgartown waterfront, effectively doubling his real estate holdings in the town center.

Dickinson promptly deeded the Starbuck Neck land to the town. Carroll donated one of his new properties, now called The Anchors, to the Edgartown Council on Aging.

Bob Carroll felt, during his decade-long battle with Edgartown's campaigning editor, the pain and futility of trying to carry an argument against a man who buys his ink by the barrel. In fact, the experience prompted him to buy his own barrel. In 1984 Carroll assembled a consortium of Island businessmen and established a new weekly newspa

2006
– TO –
2014

1890s view to the Harbor View from the walking bridge to the Edgartown Lighthouse.

THE MAN FROM ANOTHER ISLAND AND HIS GOOD IDEA

2006–2014

An experienced sailor with a savvy understanding of both the sea and business takes over the hotel and begins a long-range plan for the future.

No one was in a more perfect position to appreciate the uniqueness of the Harbor View, or to seize the opportunity to buy it, than Alan Worden.

A native of Mattapoisett, near Cape Cod, Worden had grown up enjoying the seaside and learning to sail on Sunfish and Sailfish boats. "When you learn to sail a small boat singlehandedly as a young person," he would later reflect, "you can gain so much confidence."

Worden came away from that early experience with a lifelong love of sailing—he and his then-wife, Nicole, took a year off in 1999 and 2000 to sail their forty-six-foot sloop from Nantucket to New Zealand, a voyage of nearly fourteen thousand miles.

Those childhood years by the seaside instilled a passion for this part of the world and an appreciation for the way architecture evokes a place and a style of life. "Buildings can really speak to you beyond their physicality," says Worden, who majored in architectural studies at Hobart College and went on to earn a master's degree in real estate development from Columbia University's Graduate School of Architecture, Planning and Historic Preservation.

Worden's career had prepared him amply for the challenge of taking on the Harbor View in 2006. Before his fourteen-thousand-mile sailing trip—an adventure he calls a seminal event in his life—he spent ten years affiliated with the Guggenheim family of New York, focusing on real estate

IN THE SHINGLE-STYLE
DESIGN OF THE HISTORIC
HARBOR VIEW, AND IN ITS
SPECTACULAR SITING ON
THE BLUFF AT STARBUCK
NECK, ALAN WORDEN SAW
A CLASSIC PIECE OF NEW
ENGLAND ARCHITECTURE
THAT EVOKES THE
SUMMERTIME SPIRIT OF
FAMILY AND FRIENDS,
AFTERNOON SAILING, AND
EVENING CLAMBAKES.

*But when Scout purchased the hotel its
simple and strong shingle-style
architecture had become unfocused as
previous owners had muddied the
architectural waters with Victorian
decoration. Worden met with neighbors,
town selectmen, and local regulators to
effect the changes necessary to restore it
to its original grandeur.*

investments and serving as a founder and managing director of the Guggenheim Realty Funds Management, LLC.

After his sailing adventure, he spent two years as a director of Wells Hill Partners, a real estate investment banking firm with a multibillion-dollar national practice, then settled on Nantucket and began several business ventures of his own. He founded Windwalker Real Estate in 2002; cofounded the Westmoor Club, a private field club on a twelve-acre Nantucket campus; and in 2004, created Scout Real Estate Capital with a focus on developing unique leisure opportunities for sophisticated travelers.

Worden worked with Masood Bhatti, who had been a classmate in the graduate school at Columbia and was then a managing director at Lehman Brothers, to secure financing for the 2006 purchase of the Harbor View and Kelley House.

It's no accident that two of Worden's ventures, Scout and Windwalker, were named after favorite boats. *Windwalker* was the yacht that carried the Wordens halfway around the world; *Scout* was the dinghy that took them exploring into harbor towns along their way. Worden, who went on to the serious pursuit of competitive yacht racing, says he's learned important lessons from that sport. In 2008 he told an interviewer from the magazine, *Commercial Property Executive*, "No one wins or loses a race single-handedly, although the big-ego sailors think

Boats from the Edgartown Yacht Club are beached near the hotel.

Owner Alan Worden spent months meeting with townspeople to understand the Harbor View's place on the Vineyard.

it's all about them. At Scout, we make it clear to everybody in the firm that you have to leave your ego at the door. We never care who has the right idea—we always care what is the right idea."

Bhatti, who had sailed with Worden and who was backing Scout through his financial firm, told the same interviewer, "I've never seen Alan lose his cool, whether on the boat or in business. He allows people to make mistakes and empowers them to make decisions."

Says Robin Kirk, the president of Scout Hotels, "Alan has this incredibly clear vision of places that feel right and can be made better by investment, and a clearer sense of what they can be. Edgartown is one of those places in the world, because of its unique setting, and at the Harbor View, the view is almost everything. It's not just what you look at, the buildings—it's what you look out at. Alan got that, and purchased the enterprise."

**TWO THINGS
ALAN WORDEN BELIEVES:**

Vacationers want authenticity
and a connection to community.

Time is the most precious
aspect of vacation.

Investor Masood Bhatti and his family enjoy a summer day at the Harbor View.

An important aspect of Worden's approach at Scout Hotels, the management arm of Scout Capital, has been his intense focus on research aimed at understanding the habits and practices of wealthy, vacationing baby boomers. After acquiring the Harbor View, Scout Hotels researched four thousand recent guests of the hotel—and came away with important insights.

First, Worden says, was the discovery that vacationers want authenticity, a sense that the place where they're staying has a connection with a real community. "Scout recognizes its responsibility to respond to and reinvest in the communities where we operate," he says. "Our hotels seek to involve themselves in local events, from hosting art shows with area artists to promoting locally sourced cuisine in our restaurant."

The second insight, says Worden: "The most precious commodity we all have is time." Guests at the Harbor View, like many of Edgartown's seasonal residents, have the financial wherewithal to spend their leisure time anywhere in the world—and they have chosen this place. Scout's focus at the Harbor View, he says, is to create a vacation environment where the service doesn't merely respond to the customer's needs, but anticipates them—an environment that harks back to the *Vineyard Gazette*'s description of summer life here in 1896: "A week at the Harbor View is said to be one long day of comfort and content."

IN ITS FIRST YEAR
MANAGING THE HARBOR
VIEW, SCOUT HOTELS
EMBARKED ON A ROUND
OF IMPROVEMENTS THAT
INVOLVED NEW
LANDSCAPING, REDESIGN OF
THE LOBBY, RENOVATION OF
THE FRONT PORCH, AND
THE COMPLETE REDESIGN OF
TWO OF THE CAPTAIN'S
COTTAGES BEHIND THE
MAIN HOTEL.

Leading the exterior renovation was the New York–based architect Douglas Wright, whom Worden describes as "the best shingle-style architect in the world." Linda Woodrum, whose work is regularly featured in the HGTV cable channel's Dream Home projects, led the redesign of interior spaces. Hart|Howerton, the international architectural firm based in New York and San Francisco, provided master planning for improvements to the function rooms, addition of a spa, and construction of the completely renovated Captain's Cottages.

SCOUT'S PLAN FOR THE HARBOR VIEW

Chief among the challenges of making the Harbor View a sustainable business, Worden and his management team understood from the outset, was the sheer value of the real estate involved. Purchasing the hotel in 2006 had cost about $35 million, and any business plan needed to take the cost of the mortgage with Lehman Brothers into account.

"Alan's model," says Kirk, "was to bring the Harbor View back, making it more true to its location in terms of design and function—but in order for that to happen, the financial underpinnings have to be strong enough to support the investment. The logical model today is this condominium hotel model, which makes for a healthy hotel through the sale of real estate to wealthy investors who want a stake in the town but don't want all the hassles typically associated with owning a second home.

"Interestingly enough, the hotel's layout—with the grand hotel up front and the cottages scattered around these gorgeous lawns—makes for an ideal way of doing just that."

Announcing the completion of that first round of improvements in May 2007, Worden gave the first public intimation of his plan for the future of the Harbor View. "We've received more than a few emails and telephone inquiries from long-term guests who have asked about owning a hotel guest suite at the Harbor View," he said. "We are actively considering offering ownership of hotel suites. But first and foremost, the Harbor View will remain a hotel, and our focus is on improving the hotel and resort experience for our guests."

PLANNING FOR A MAKEOVER

For the next phase in what Scout Hotels envisioned as a $77 million makeover of the Harbor View Hotel, permits were needed from Edgartown and also from the Martha's Vineyard Commission, the regional regulatory agency with broad powers to approve, deny, or attach conditions to any of its building plans.

The MVC's charter empowers the agency to review Developments of Regional Impact, or DRIs. When Scout presented the commission with its plans for the Harbor View early in 2008, its project was assigned DRI No. 614. It was fortunate for Alan Worden that his colleagues at Scout thrive on complexity. Watching the way the team ushered the Harbor View project through the MVC's lengthy review, one observer remarked that if they enjoyed such difficult work, they must also enjoy root canals.

The MVC's review of the Scout plan for the Harbor View was bracketed by acknowledgments of the hotel's impor-

tance, both to Island history and as an ongoing part of the Island economy. The staff report introducing the project in April 2008 identified several key issues for the commission to consider, first among which was: "The hotel is an Island landmark. How will these changes affect its appearance?" The agency's approval of the project, four months later, concluded, "The Commission finds that the proposed renovations to the Harbor View Hotel, which has been located at this site since 1891, would represent a beneficial upgrading to this facility which is important to the character and economy of Edgartown and the Island as a whole."

As part of its application to the MVC, Scout Real Estate Capital commissioned an analysis of the Harbor View's impacts on the Island economy. The analysis concluded that after renovations, the Harbor View and Kelley House hotels would together support about 400 jobs and generate $10 million in annual household income on Martha's Vineyard.

The MVC's approval of the Harbor View project, a twelve-page document handed down on August 8, 2008, included a long list of conditions. Six public hearings had preceded that decision, and the paper trail ran to hundreds of pages.

KEY ELEMENTS OF THE PROJECT
as approved by the Martha's Vineyard Commission included:

CHANGE IN THE HOTEL'S OWNERSHIP TO A HOTEL/CONDO STRUCTURE IN WHICH INDIVIDUAL SUITES IN THE CAPTAIN'S COTTAGES WOULD BE SOLD TO PRIVATE OWNERS, BUT WITH PROVISIONS FOR MOST OF THOSE SUITES TO SPEND MOST OF THE YEAR IN THE HOTEL'S RENTAL PROGRAM.

EXPANSION AND RENOVATION OF THE HARBOR VIEW'S FACILITIES FOR GROUPS AND LARGE FUNCTIONS.

CONSTRUCTION OF A NEW SWIMMING POOL, A FITNESS CENTER AND DAY SPA, AND A CHILDREN'S PROGRAM ROOM.

DEMOLITION OF BOB CARROLL'S MOTEL BUILDING BEHIND THE HARBOR VIEW, NOW CALLED THE MAYHEW BUILDING, AND ITS REPLACEMENT WITH FIVE SMALLER COTTAGES. WORDEN EXPLAINED, IN AN INTERVIEW INTRODUCING HIS PLANS FOR THE HOTEL, THAT THE MOTEL UNITS DIDN'T FIT THE HIGH-END RESORT THE HARBOR VIEW HAD BECOME. "CONSUMERS TODAY WANT LARGER, NICER ROOMS," HE SAID. THE PLAN APPROVED BY THE MVC WOULD INCREASE THE TOTAL SQUARE FOOTAGE OF BUILDINGS AT THE HARBOR VIEW BY ABOUT 20 PERCENT, BUT CUT THE NUMBER OF RENTAL UNITS FROM 116 TO 68.

With all the necessary permits in hand, Worden and the Scout management team were preparing for the first phase of their building program and readying the Captain's Cottages for presentation to prospective buyers when suddenly—five weeks after winning the MVC's green light —the hotel's financial underpinnings collapsed.

SUDDENLY, THE LENDERS ARE FROM STOCKHOLM

On the morning of September 15, 2008, Lehman Brothers Holdings Inc., the fourth-largest financial firm in the United States, filed for bankruptcy protection. It was the largest bankruptcy in U.S. history, an event later nicknamed "Lehmangeddon" by finance industry pundits—and it marked the beginning of the global financial crisis that would play out over the next few years.

For Scout Hotels, there was a wait while the dust settled around the collapse of the financial giant that had held the loans on the Harbor View property. Masood Bhatti, freshly out of a job at Lehman Brothers, joined Scout Capital as a full partner with Worden and began the process of figuring out where those Harbor View loans had gone.

"It was just chaos for a while," recalls Bhatti, "because these were all repo transactions. Finally we figured out that the Harbor View was with Swedbank. Even Swedbank didn't know they had the loan."

"So Lehman goes away," says Kirk, "and in comes a new financial partner—out of nowhere—called Swedbank. This came as something of a surprise to Alan, and as something of a surprise to Swedbank too, to tell the truth."

Having done business with Lehman Brothers for many years, Swedbank, one of the largest banking institutions in Sweden, found itself holding $1.35 billion in loans covering some seventy real estate assets in the United States—and among them, as it turned out, was the Harbor View Hotel.

Kirk acknowledges that even if Scout had been free to market the condominium units in the fall of 2008, selling them might have been difficult in the depths of that real estate recession. "They did invest in the hotel," says Kirk, "allowing us to renovate the Mayhew Building. But Swedbank said, no, don't sell any cottage units—for reasons known only to Swedbank. This was especially odd since the first phase of suites were spoken for."

Without a plan to raise funds from the sale of condominium units, the $77 million renovation of the Harbor View Hotel was put on hold. And Masood Bhatti, Alan Worden's partner at Scout, began working to bring control of the Harbor View back to local investors who understood Edgartown, appreciated the hotel's importance as an Island landmark, and would support the best plan for its long-term sustainability.

SWEDBANK HAD NO MORE INTEREST IN OWNING A RESORT HOTEL IN EDGARTOWN THAN THE MANAGERS OF THE HARBOR VIEW HAD IN BEING ANSWERABLE TO ABSENTEE LENDERS AN OCEAN AWAY. AND ONE OF THE FIRST INSTRUCTIONS SWEDBANK GAVE TO THE SCOUT TEAM WAS TO PUT A HOLD ON THE KEY ELEMENT OF THEIR MANAGEMENT PLAN, THE SALE OF CONDOMINIUM SUITES IN THE NEWLY RESTORED CAPTAIN'S COTTAGES.

THE HARBOR VIEW HOSTS BETWEEN TWENTY AND TWENTY-FIVE WEDDINGS A YEAR, EVERYTHING FROM THE VERY FORMAL BLACK-TIE EVENT TO THE MORE CASUAL BUT STILL BEAUTIFUL WEDDINGS. BUT HISTORY TELLS US THE TRADITION STARTED IN 1948.

1948: THE FIRST WEDDING

It's hard to imagine the Harbor View Hotel today without the festivity of the wedding parties that fill its calendar each spring and fall. But when Eileen Walker Sibley, granddaughter of hotel founder Thomas Walker, was married on September 11, 1948, the reception at the Harbor View was big news.

"One of the most beautiful weddings Edgartown has seen took place Saturday afternoon at 2," reported the *Vineyard Gazette*, "when Miss Eileen Walker Sibley, daughter of Mr. and Mrs. Luther Morrill Sibley of Edgartown, became the bride of Rupert Henry Robinson, son of Mr. and Mrs. Rupert West Robinson of Worcester."

The Congregational church was packed with family and friends for the ceremony performed by Rev. William Thompson. Afterward, all repaired to the music room of the Harbor View, where bride and bridegroom received their guests beside the grand fireplace decorated with greenery and flowers.

Eileen Walker Robinson, who lives now in Oak Bluffs, believes this was the first wedding reception ever held at the Harbor View. "The hotel was kept open an extra week after Labor Day," she says, "just for the party." The only blemish on the day, as she recalls it, was that her mother was unable to attend the party, convalescing from a recent hospital stay in an upstairs room at the hotel.

Wedding gifts for the couple had been arranged on tables in the spacious music room, which was decorated by Mrs. Charles Center, wife of the Harbor View manager, with white gladioli, white pom-pom chrysanthemums, gypsophila, and greens. The tiered wedding cake, made at the Harbor View, was topped with the traditional bridal figures. Miss Joyce West caught the bride's bouquet.

Eileen Walker Robinson changed into a beige gabardine suit with brown orchid corsage for the couple's departure, leaving the Harbor View grounds through showers of confetti to a car which took them down to the harbor, to a seaplane piloted by Steve Gentle. The plane circled the hotel, dipping low over the window of the room in which Mrs. Sibley was resting, and then flew on to Boston.

— The —
ANNIVERSARY ISETTA

When Victoria Danberg was growing up in Edgartown, her father, the late Victor A. Danberg, bought her a 1960 Isetta micro-car, and she spent the rest of her high school years scooting around the Island in the tiny egg-shaped vehicle. "The family story," says her husband, Dr. John Ficarelli, "is that her father got that car because he figured that with only two cylinders, she wouldn't be able to get it above the Island speed limit of 45 miles per hour."

When Victoria went to college, the family sold the Isetta to a young woman who soon crashed and wrecked it. "Vic regretted losing that car for a long time," says John, "and whenever we'd see one at a car show, she'd reminisce about it."

John and Vic were married at St. Andrew's Church on August 18, 1973, and their reception party was held at the Harbor View Hotel. That day, recalls John, "One of my cousins went to the management of the hotel and asked if he could buy two place-settings of their china for us to remember the day by. They gave him two settings, and we've kept that china in a sideboard ever since then."

In 2013 John decided to see if he could find an Isetta and surprise his wife with it as a 40th anniversary gift. He finally found a bright red 1958 model in Kennebunk, Maine, purchased it, and arranged for its transport—on the back of a pickup truck—to the family's summer place in Edgartown.

On the day of the anniversary celebration, John's sons drove the Isetta to the hotel. "The Harbor View was very accommodating," he says. "They actually put cones out right in front of the hotel to block off a space for the car."

When John and Victoria drove up to the hotel for their anniversary dinner at Water Street Restaurant, there was the Isetta, wrapped in a big bow. "But Vic didn't put two and two together right away," says John. "She saw the car, and we went over to look at it. She was saying, oh look, it's an Isetta like the one I had! That's when I handed her the keys."

The staff at Water Street was just wonderful, John says, the way they helped with arrangements for the anniversary dinner. He'd packed the 1973 place-settings carefully in bubble wrap and delivered them to the hotel in advance. "So when Vic sat down at her place, there was the china from her wedding day.

"It all worked out very well. I think we really were able to pull off a complete surprise."

2014

Twilight on the Vineyard, with calm seas and a bright moon.

HOMECOMING

2014

A new owner's group with strong ties to the community—including some neighbors on Starbuck Neck—forms around the understanding that the Harbor View "is a very special place."

With the Harbor View's mortgage now held by a distant banking firm unwilling to support Scout's business plan, it was time to negotiate a deal. Making that deal—bringing the Harbor View Hotel back under local control—took more than three years.

During this period, Masood Bhatti of Scout Capital formed a new enterprise, Harborview Investors LLC, and reached out to an old Columbia University classmate and friend who was also a well-connected member of the Edgartown summer community.

The investors whom Bhatti ultimately pulled together are, he says, "a unique group of people who understand that the Harbor View is a very special place, and they want to make sure it thrives and does well for the community." The friend and former classmate who helped him build Harborview Investors is Peter Lawson-Johnston. Recalls Bhatti, "I reached out to Peter and said, 'I'm not really known on Martha's Vineyard.' He's the one who gave me names and introduced me to people."

One of the principals in Harborview Investors is Drew Conway, whose two residences at 67 and 71 North Water Street offer commanding views of Edgartown Harbor, from Tower Hill to the lighthouse and the Harbor View Hotel. Conway, whose family has been summering on the Vineyard for two decades, immediately understood the need for a local investor group, and he had a personal affection for

A snowy winter's day on the Vineyard showcases the hotel in a very different way.

the Harbor View dating back to the day when he and his wife, Kimberly, were married at the hotel.

"We're a pretty close-knit group here on the Island," says Conway.

"A lot of us belong to the same clubs and organizations, and when we see each other we talk about the Island. When it was brought to my attention that the Harbor View was in a bit of a stress mode financially, given the Lehman situation and Swedbank not really being interested in investing in it, I took an interest in that. Not to make a lot of money or strip-mine the hotel—but to preserve this great asset of the town of Edgartown."

Another member of the Harbor View's core owner group is David Brush, who with his wife, Karen, and their family have been summering in Edgartown for the better part of three decades. Real estate is Brush's business as managing partner of the Brookfield Property Group, a global firm with more than $175 billion in assets under management.

"My wife teases me," says Brush, "that every time we go on holiday, I end up spending time looking at real estate or reading about what's going on locally. It's something I can't seem to avoid."

When Bhatti presented him with the opportunity to invest in the Harbor View, Brush recalls thinking, *That would be an interesting thing to become involved with.* "And it wasn't something that was all about the finances. To me, the Harbor View was always more than a piece of real estate. It's something that is iconic, such a big part of the Edgartown community."

Over the years, the Brush family's summer stays in Edgartown have lengthened, and their ties in the community have deepened. "Our family's long-term plan now," he says, "is to have this be our primary residence. When the day comes when I finally hang up my cleats, this is the place I'd like to retire to."

And with that deepening connection, says Brush, comes a sense of responsibility to support a healthy Island community. In addition to their stewardship of the Harbor View, the Brushes have been supporters of Island nonprofits from

"This is a real place, not a playground, and we don't want to lose that."

the Farm Institute to the YMCA, from the Martha's Vineyard Hospital to Community Services.

On May 23, 2012, with its new investor group in place, it was time for the transition. As managing partner of Harborview Investors, Bhatti took a $40 million mortgage with Northstar Financial Partners and bought back the hotel's loan from Swedbank. For the first time since the late summer of 2008, Scout Hotels was free to pursue its plans for a sustainable future at the Harbor View.

With the issue of the hotel's ownership finally resolved, Bhatti left Scout Capital in September 2012 to join a number of former Lehman Brothers colleagues at the financial services giant UBS. Scout Hotels, Alan Worden's management firm, now answers to Bhatti's investor group—a group with deep local ties, most of them owners of seasonal homes on North Water Street and elsewhere in Edgartown.

Scout leadership believes, "When an enterprise like the Harbor View Hotel works well, like so many things, it's done by people with a vested interest in the community."

—— VOICES ——

Left to Right: David Brush,
Drew Conway (center), and Masood Bhatti

DREW CONWAY

"The Island needs the support of its summer residents. It's not really sustainable without that. And here's this beautiful hotel up the street that needs a group of guys, ideally civic-minded, in-town people, who can support it and bring it back to its roots of being a pillar of the Edgartown community.

"This hotel is such a core piece of the fabric of this Island. That's why it's so important to have the right caretakers— people who get that. From my perspective, it's an honor to have the opportunity to be a part of the ownership of the Harbor View Hotel. The responsibility I feel about that, I think it's shared throughout our whole group. We really do love this place."

Drew and Kim Conway with their son,
Alex, on the porch of the Harbor View
for their wedding on November 7, 1992.

ROCKING IN PARADISE

Each of the hotel's more than fifty classic rocking chairs gets a light sanding and a fresh coat of glossy Majestic Blue oil-based paint every May, and then at midsummer the painting crew begins rotating chairs off the porches, ten at a time, for touch-ups. Donnie Ethier, the Harbor View's engineering coordinator, can tell you by the grain of a rocker's wood, the shape of the stretcher dowels, and the slight curve of the back slats that it's one of the original chairs dating to the earliest years of the hotel.

A RENAISSANCE OF COMMUNITY OUTREACH

Under Scout Hotels' management, and with the support of its new ownership group, the Harbor View has reconnected with the Island community in a way that harks back to its earliest years as a center for festive events in Edgartown.

The Harbor View collaborated with *Arts & Ideas* magazine in October 2012 to create Arts*Island, a five-day celebration of art at the hotel. The walls of the entire first floor were covered with art, and the week's programs included films, parties, art classes, and a children's carnival.

In the spring of 2013 the Harbor View reached out to the Animal Shelter of Martha's Vineyard, inviting the organization to hold its fifth annual Celebration of Animals at the hotel in June.

The Harbor View has invited the Martha's Vineyard Film Festival to expand its calendar of Chilmark events to include public screenings at the hotel, and in August 2012 the hotel served for the first time as a Down-Island venue for the Martha's Vineyard Book Festival.

Add New Year's fireworks in the winter and live music on the summer lawns, Pecha Kucha nights sponsored by the Martha's Vineyard Museum in the conference rooms, gourmet programs for foodies like the Swine & Dine Gala Dinner that culminates a week of study by visiting chefs—and you can fill a calendar with all the events the Harbor View is offering to the community.

COMING BACK

"In June of 1985, my wife, Carin, and I enjoyed part of our honeymoon at the Harbor View. We wanted to make our honeymoon special and where we stayed was important to us. We were young and didn't have much money. We decided that we could afford to stay at the Harbor View for the first half of our weeklong honeymoon. Then we moved up the street to another place, not quite as special.

"We so loved the Harbor View that we continued to walk each day back to the hotel, just to sit by the pool. The staff, which we had come to know during our brief stay, made us feel so welcome, even though we weren't even staying there.

"We are older now and have a bit more money, so the next time we visit Martha's Vineyard, I think we can afford to stay the whole week at the Harbor View Hotel."

DAVID BARBOUR
Bridgeport, Connecticut

Elizabeth Rothwell, who grew up on the Island and has been the Harbor View's director of marketing and events since 2011, has been on the hotel staff full-time since the spring of 2007, just after Scout Hotels took over.

Her dual role overseeing marketing and programs positions her perfectly, Rothwell says.

"Now when someone comes to me with a great idea like the Martha's Vineyard Book Festival, I can say, 'Let's do this'—because it's good for the hotel, it's a good thing for the community. And I have support from Scout Hotels to do that."

An example of the Harbor View's outreach is the Celebration of Animals event in June 2013, which brought dozens of dogs (including Rothwell's own Yorkshire terrier, Izzie), a goat, and even a pair of llamas to the hotel. "We turned the Harbor View pet-friendly a couple of years ago, and a lot of people still don't know about that," she says.

"In the winter, when we were brainstorming ideas for some hotel-sponsored events, we came up with the plan trying to get the word out about our pet-friendly policy while also helping the Vineyard Animal Shelter get their message out."

Rothwell talked to Greg Orcutt, manager of Vineyard radio station WMVY, who serves with her on the board of the Martha's Vineyard Chamber of Commerce and is also a member of the animal shelter's board. He jumped at the opportunity to hold the shelter's annual event at the hotel.

"Everyone at the Harbor View just made us feel so welcome. A man in a black dog suit led a parade around the Edgartown Light, and the hotel provided all kinds of special cookies and treats. We really felt we were the focus of that moment at the Harbor View. And we got great play in both Island newspapers, which is something that's never happened before."

—A NICE PLACE—
TO SPEND A NIGHT

"THE CENTERPIECE OF THIS HISTORIC HOTEL IS A GRAY-SHINGLE, 1891 VICTORIAN BUILDING WITH WRAPAROUND VERANDA AND A GAZEBO. ACCOMMODATIONS INCLUDE FINE DECOR AND PLUSH IN-ROOM AMENITIES. A BEACH, GOOD FOR WALKING, STRETCHES THREE-FOURTHS MILE FROM THE HOTEL'S DOCK. THE EXTENSIVE CHILDREN'S SUMMER PROGRAM HAS A FULL ROSTER OF ACTIVITIES FOR KIDS."

Fodor's

Through the years, the rooms at the Harbor View have been bragged about—and constantly changed. At one point, the hotel touted that it had an automatic sprinkler system and telephones in every room. Today, it is likely to brag about its plush robes and wireless connections.

Today, the hotel has thirty-seven rooms in the main building, many with water views of the harbor, lighthouse, and beaches. The Governor Mayhew rooms, the section added in the 1960s, have garden and pool views. And in all cases, the hotel continues to brag about the care it gives to its guests—and, of course, the proximity to what a brochure in the 1950s described as a place "where the air is clean, the water is crystal clear, the beaches have no hot dog stands, and there isn't a billboard to be found."

FROM THE HARBOR VIEW TO THE WHITE HOUSE

FOOD HAS BEEN A PART OF THE HARBOR VIEW FROM THE VERY BEGINNING, WHEN FOR $2 OR $3, YOU COULD GET THREE MEALS A DAY. A STANDARD OF EXCELLENT CUISINE HAS BEEN A HALLMARK OF THE HARBOR VIEW HOTEL—CERTAINLY NEVER MORE THAN TODAY.

In the White House kitchen: Executive Chef Henry Haller puts finishing touches on food for visiting dignitaries and heads of state.

But when Alfred Hall bought the hotel in 1948, he went over the top.

Alfred and Marjorie Hall searched far and wide for the hotel's next chef. In the end, they drove across the country to interview and recruit a young chef who was then working in Arizona. His name was Henry Haller, a native of Switzerland who trained at the famed Park Hotel in Davos before immigrating to Canada and then to the United States after the Second World War.

The Halls chose well. Their daughter, Charlotte, still remembers the Sunday feasts Chef Haller served at the Harbor View, the buffet tables laden with food and decorated with his gleaming ice sculptures. Recalls their son, Buzz, "His cuisine was basically New England with French undertones."

At the Harbor View, Chef Haller met Carole Itjem from Brooklyn, a mathematics major from Bucknell University who was waitressing for the summer in the hotel dining room. They married and raised four children.

After a decade at the Harbor View, Chef Haller went on to work as head cook at the fashionable Sheraton East Hotel in New York City, where he commanded a staff of fifty. From the Sheraton he was recruited by Lady Bird Johnson and went on to a twenty-two-year stint—serving the presidential administrations of Johnson, Nixon, Ford, Carter, and Reagan—as executive chef at the White House.

THE COOKIES

ON A SUMMER'S DAY, THE HARBOR VIEW KITCHEN WILL MAKE AND SELL DOZENS OF CHOCOLATE
CHIP COOKIES THROUGH ITS RESTAURANTS AND ROOM SERVICE. THEY ARE GOOEY AND DELICIOUS,
AND A FAVORITE OF GUESTS AND STAFF ALIKE.

HARBOR VIEW CHOCOLATE CHIP COOKIES

Yield: 2 dozen cookies

INGREDIENTS

½ CUP ALL-PURPOSE FLOUR

½ CUP BREAD FLOUR

1 TSP. BAKING SODA

¾ TSP. KOSHER SALT

1½ STICKS UNSALTED BUTTER

½ CUP GRANULATED SUGAR

½ CUP LIGHT BROWN SUGAR

2 WHOLE EGGS

1½ TSP. VANILLA EXTRACT

1½ CUPS CHOCOLATE CHIPS

DIRECTIONS

1. Preheat the oven to 350°F.

2. Sift the all-purpose flour, bread flour, baking soda, and salt. Set aside.

3. Cream the butter, granulated sugar, and brown sugar until light and fluffy.
   Scrape the bowl.

4. Gradually add the eggs one at a time, mixing until incorporated and
   scraping down the bowl after each addition.

5. Add the vanilla and mix until incorporated.

6. Add the dry ingredients and mix until just incorporated. Scrape the bowl.

7. Add the chocolate chips; mix until combined.

8. Scoop tablespoon-size portions of batter onto parchment-lined sheet pans,
   about 2 inches apart. Bake at 350°F for 12 to 15 minutes or until golden brown.

"When you're sitting on that porch in those old rockers, and you have a drink in your hand, there's not another place in the world where you'd rather be at that moment. You are in paradise; you couldn't be coaxed off that rocker for anything."

DREW CONWAY, LEADING MEMBER OF THE INVESTMENT GROUP THAT HAS BROUGHT CONTROL OF THE HARBOR VIEW BACK INTO THE HANDS OF PEOPLE WHO UNDERSTAND ITS HISTORY AND IMPORTANCE

THE END: TO BE CONTINUED

*Perhaps the most remarkable thing
about this story of the Harbor View Hotel
is that it doesn't have an ending.*

Over its history of nearly 125 years, the Harbor View has seen bankruptcy, fire, economic cycles of boom and bust, and the transformation of Martha's Vineyard from a sleepy community of subsistence farmers and fishing folk into a world-class resort destination and the summer home of U.S. presidents. Again and again the Harbor View faced moments of crisis when the easiest way out would have been to knock the hotel down, break the property up, and sell it for private summer residences. But each time, people stepped in who saw something worth saving in this property overlooking the entrance to Edgartown Harbor. And so the enterprise has endured.

What exactly is it that gives the Harbor View such a special resonance that generation after Edgartown generation have invested their resources and energy in it?

Certainly one part of the Harbor View's value is its primacy in Edgartown's history. Edgartown today has many inns and hotels, but only one of them can be the very first, and the Harbor View is that one. Even though few know the whole remarkable story of the Harbor View—and this book is an effort to redress that—the historic resonance of the place somehow remains impossible to ignore.

Another undeniable aspect of the Harbor View's magic is its setting, the way it fits so perfectly on the bluffs of Starbuck Neck with its porches overlooking the grand vista of Chappaquiddick, the Edgartown lighthouse, the outer and inner harbors, and the village.

However you slice the story of the Harbor View Hotel—whichever era in its history you examine—this remains the story of a hotel defined, in large part, by harbor and town it looks out upon. The people of Edgartown understood that in the winter of 1890 and 1891 when they chose to name the new hotel for its expansive view. And they still understand it.

NIS KILDEGAARD
Author

ALISON SHAW
Photographer

Nis Kildegaard was born in Iowa, raised in Chicago, educated at Yale University, and came to Martha's Vineyard in 1981 from *The New York Times* to become news editor of the *Vineyard Gazette.* He held that post for twenty-four years until 2004, when he built a second career as reference librarian at the Edgartown Public Library (which he prefers to call the Edgartown Dept. of Neat, Free Stuff). He writes a monthly op-ed column for the *Martha's Vineyard Times,* produces annual reports and newsletters for several of the Island's major nonprofit organizations, is an avid bicyclist and photographer, sings in the Island Community Chorus, and enjoys tinkering with all things mechanical, especially antique typewriters. He lives in Edgartown with his wife, Carolyn, a counselor at Martha's Vineyard Community Services, and their pet box turtle, Phoebe.

Alison Shaw is a Martha's Vineyard–based photographer who specializes in fine art and editorial photography. The Island has provided the primary inspiration and subject matter for her since 1979, when she came here "just for the summer" after she had graduated from Smith College. Alison's photos grace the pages of innumerable books, magazines, and newspapers. She has now collaborated with Vineyard Stories on seven books featuring the Island. She teaches workshops around the country. The Alison Shaw Gallery, which she co-owns with her partner, Sue Dawson, is located in an old single-engine firehouse in the heart of the Arts District in Oak Bluffs. She presents regularly changing shows there. You can view more of her work at www.alisonshaw.com. Alison and Nis worked together for twenty years at the *Vineyard Gazette*, and this is their first book collaboration.